THE PARADOXES OF DEMOCRACY

THE PARADOXES OF DEMOCRACY

Edited by

GUY HERMET
HELGIO TRINDADE

GIAN PUBLISHING HOUSE
DELHI-110007

GIAN PUBLISHING HOUSE
29/6, Shakti Nagar, Delhi-110007,
Ph. 7213053

ISBN 81-212-0219-1

Printed in India

Published by Mrs. Gayatri Garg for Gian Publishing House
29/6, Shakti Nagar, Delhi-110007

Printed at
Bharat Enterprises, Delhi

EDITORS' FOREWORD

The birth and progress of democratic government are not the fruits of philanthropy or ideological imagination only. They also stem from the interactions of economic, cultural and political factors which are shaping the background and the environment of democracy-building in each historical circumstance. And they depend all the same on the strategic capability of the "political entrepreneurs" who are facing the obstacles which always lie on the path to democracy.

In short, the study of democracy-making must take into consideration a paradoxical situation *i.e.*, the good intentions of the convinced democrats, and the perverse effects of facts or situations which have nothing in common with these intentions. In other terms again, the analysts of democracy-building must first of all be conscious of a series of paradoxes. And so must they in both cases of the slow emergence of the old European representative regimes, and of the current path to democracy in the "South", which is considered in greater detail in this book.

This volume offers for a revisitation of some of these paradoxes. It happens to be the product of an academic meeting which took place in New Delhi under the auspices of the Committee of Political Sociology, on the occasion of the XIth Congress of the International Sociological Association held in August, 1986. Though some of its contributors were then discovering India for the first time, all of them had certainly this country in mind during their discussions, and while they were revising the last draft of their respective chapter. However, they stood on the decision of maintaining a distance in front of the impressive Indian example.

Hence, in the first part of this book focus has been kept on general theoretical perspectives dealing with diverse aspects of the paradoxical democratic power. Chapter I, presented by Franco Crespi, refers to the very paradox of power in itself, in its links with democratic politics. Chapter II, written by Peter Ronald de Souza, considers the ever conflicting relationship between science, values and democratic theory. And Gisele De Meur, revisits in Chapter III the paradoxical and perverse effects of electoral laws on party systems, in the light of the last contributions about this controversial question.

The second part contains a collection of comparative views, or case studies on democracy-building as it is currently occurring in different regions of the Third World. Helgio Trindade's opening chapter analyzes its first sequence, which derives from the primary process of State-building, in the neighbouring but contrasting Brazilian and Argentinian examples. In Chapter V, a French scholar—Max-Jean Zins—scrutinizes with a fresh perception the paradox of democracy in India. Is India an exception in the Third World? And finally, the last two Chapters share a comparative perspective. In Chapter VI, Dirk Berg-Schlosser examines the possible paths to democracy in Third World countries. The concluding chapter by Guy Hermet argues against the idea that democracy is necessarily conquered by the people. In other words, it sustains the paradox that an authoritarian democratization is an unpleasant but verified hypothesis in the recent time.

We hope this book will reach some of the many citizens who are concerned about the enlargement of the physical and moral frontiers of democracy in today's world. If it helps in stimulating public and academic debates, we will feel that it has served its purpose. However, readers may assess the merits of the views expressed in this volume in the light of their own experience and conviction.

Paris, Porto Alegre
January 1987

GUY HERMET
HELGIO TRINDADE

CONTRIBUTORS

PR. DR. DIRK BERG-SCHOSSER is professor ar the Institute of Political Science at Phillips University in Marburg, Western Germany. He has contributed a number of studies on politics in the Third World, and political culture in Germany.

PR. FRANCO CRESPI is Director of the Institute of Social Studies at the University of Perugia, Italy. His field of specialisation is political theory.

GISELE DE MEUR is a mathematician and political scientist at the Centre of Mathematical Economics of Brussels Free University, in Belgium. Her particular interests presently lies in electoral systems.

D. GUY HERMET is Research Director at the National Foundation for Political Science in Paris, France. His recent works are focused on late democracy-building in Europe and Latin America.

PETER RONALD DE SOUZA is attached to the Department of Social Sciences, University of Sussex, Brighton, England. He specializes in political theory.

PR. DR. HELGIO TRINDADE is currently Vice-Rector of the Federal University of Rio Grande do Sul in Porto Alegre,

Brazil. As a political scientist, he has written extensively on State Building in South America.

DR. MAX-JEAN ZINS is a French political scientist with specialisation in Indian affairs. As a member of the CNRS-ORSTOM, he is at present working in Delhi.

CONTENTS

Part I

Theoretical Perspectives

1

THE PARADOX OF POWER

FRANCO CRESPI

The paradoxical character of democracy is directly connected to the paradoxical character of human society itself as a matter of fact democracy can be considered as the only political order which entirely recognizes the paradoxical character of society.

The term 'paradox' can be used in connection with democracy in many ways; but certainly one of its aspect is founded on the fact that social situation appears based on one hand on normative predictability, or on what we can consider as *determined* forms of symbolic mediation, while on the other hand society is the product of lived experience and action, that is to say of *indetermined* and ever changing needs and choices. No society is possible without some sort of consensus and a shared system of rules, but social reality is not only the result of the observance of norms but also of what some sociologists call the "functional non observance" (see Manciulli, 1986), that is to say the fact that any social organization functions only through a partial infringement of norms. As those social actors who make a protest scrupulously applying the written rules of their organization (*greve de zele* or *zeal strike*) perfectly know, without a constant adaptation of the rules or even without a relative inobservance of them, the functioning of any social system will come to a stop. This is due to the fact that norms as symbolic mediation forms are by their nature always *reductive* with respect to the complexity of lived experience: in the last analysis they will always prove inadequate to the manifold needs of social action. They will have to be changed or replaced by other norms which sooner or later will also prove inadequate and so on.

To find a *determined* order it is necessary to reduce complexity and somehow to consider as an absolute the determined form: if I want to make definite a situation and create predictability I must proceed by yes and no, black and white, mine and yours, in a clear cut way. But this is precisely the contradiction of social situation: the more determined form is also the more reductive, which means that the more reductive is also the more absolutized.

This basic contradiction, connected to the dimensions of consciousness and of symbolic mediation which characterize the human situation (see Crespi, 1985), explains why there is no final solution to the problem of society. There will never be a transparent and non-contradictory society because there will never be a symbolic order totally adequate to the complexity of human experience. This shows that those social or political theories which insist upon the perfectibility of society are intrinsically utopian: by their abstractedness they will in the last analysis tend to some sort of totalitarianism. While those theories which recognize the irreconcilable character of social situation will tend to think in terms of the possibility of constant reform, adopting a more pragmatic attitude towards the real actual social context.

While utopian totalitarian theories think in terms of *overcoming* the contradictions, democratic theories should think in terms of *managing* the contradictions of social situation. While the first type of theories pretend to possess the truth, developing dogmatic systems of knowledge (theological or "scientific"), democratic theories will always insist on the limits of human knowledge.

It is interesting to see that the theories which pretend to be wholly opposed to totalitarianism, like anarchist theories, also think in term of overcoming the contradictions, this time by *abolishing* power, establishing perfect equality, founding society on *natural* grounds, *etc.* Democratic theories thus appear as striking a middle path between the two extreme theories. On the one hand the most *determined* conception of social order, on the other hand the most *indetermined* one. Both these extremes miss the point: society in fact, as we have seen, is the locus of the *relation* between *determinacy* (predictability, consensus, order) and *indeterminacy* (unpredictable aspect of experience and practical action, conflict, disorder and one cannot go without the other.

It is on the basis of these presuppositions that I will try to show in the following pages that to the paradoxical character of society corresponds the paradoxical or ambivalent character of power, which can well be considered an essential function of social reality, a function democratic systems must know how to deal with.

1. The three dimensions of power

If we take into account the ambivalence of the relationship between determinacy and indeterminacy both at the individual level (relation between identity and non-identity) and at the social level (relation between predictability and adaptation), we can adopt a general definition of power as *the capacity to deal with the contradic ions arising in the dynamic relation between determinacy and indeterminacy.*

This capacity can be analysed at three levels: a) as an *intrinsic subjective* capacity, b) as an *extrinsic subjective* capacity and c) as an *objective structural* function.

The three levels are each one referring to a specific analytical field: the first one refers mainly to the existential dynamics of the individual and is directly connected with psychological aspects; the second one is related to the sphere of intersubjectivity and symbolic interaction and is directly connected with social psychology; the third one refers to structural and normative problems and is connected with social systems theory and other sociological aspects. Even if the term power has varied meanings in relation to each different level (*inherent capacity* at the first one; *social function* at the second one; *structure* at the third one) it is important not to lose sight of the fact that the different forms of power are all connected to the fundamental question of the capacity to deal with the contradictions of social situation. As we will see further on, the possibility to establish a connection among these different forms shows the limits of any extrinsic power, the relevance but also the ambiguity of structural power. the importance of intrinsic power in the perspective of emancipation. As a matter of fact, neither of these different dimensions are independent of each another and only a theory which recognizes their interrelations will be able to avoid the reductiveness and unidimensionality so frequent in many power theories.

Let us consider briefly each level.

1.1 The intrinsic power of the individual

As it is well known, an individual is exposed from birth to an intense process of socialization, through the cultural forms that govern every aspect of his life and particularly his relations with parents and other members of the family, the relation with the world outside, *etc*. At the moment of his birth the individual appears as totally lacking in power: the infants are totally dependent on the adult and even his capacity to recognize himself is connected to the previous recognition of the adult. The building of his identity and the ways in which he will make the experience of others and of things are mediated by the prevailing symbolic forms of his social context. The shaping of individual personality, however, is not a mere passive process. The subject is not only a *tabula rasa* on which the different physical and psychical influences of parental actions, language, symbols, social rules, patterns of behavior, material conditions, *etc.*, have an impact, but he is also a field of elaboration of such influences. The individual on the basis of his own experiences, is capable, from the first months of life, of defending himself from the social environment (see Klein, 1952). The mechanisms of defence appear as functions of a peculiar world of experience which soon will lead the subject to constitute a specific system of meanings and symbols, only partly, derived from the legacy of his social environment. The social and cultural codes, once assimilated and internalized, can be used by the subject as tools for his personal expression. Between the *internal* world of the individual, structured by social environment and personally mediated, and the *external* world of social relations there is thus a discontinuity which allows the subject to enter into a relation with his fellows through his own *identity*, while preserving his *difference*.

As a matter of fact individual identity has an ambivalent nature because it requires at the same time the subject to be *alike* the others in order to be recognized by them and to be *different* from others so as to escape anonymity and being taken for granted. Again there is an oscillation between determinacy (identity in the sens of "alike") and indeterminacy (identity in the sense of being "different"). Obviously the capacity of elaboration of an internal image of the Self is as essential to the subject as his capacity of internalizing collectively shared models and values.

In order to understand the complex constitution of the subject and the problem of identity it seems, therefore, necessary to distinguish between:

(a) the level of the subject's *personal identity* as the result of conscious and unconscious elaboration of experience, corresponding to the image the individual has of himself (see Turner, 1968); (b) the level of the subject's *social identity* corresponding to the image that the subject *gives* of himself to others in the social interaction and communication processes (see Goffman, 1959).

Obviously these two aspects of identity are interdependent since personal identity could not form without social identity and vice versa. Both personal and social identities together make up the total identity of the social actor (see Tajfel, 1972). Although both dimensions are deeply connected to the symbolic forms prevailing in the social context, the relative autonomy of personal over social identity allows the individual to use the latter as a *mask*, maintaining a typical "distance from the role" which enforces the power of the social actor (see Goffman, 1961). The *intrinsic power* of the subject can thus be defined as *the capacity of using personal and social identities without absolutizing them, but recognizing their limits and their mutual interdependence.* In fact, if the subject absolutizes his social identity he will be totally dependent from his social role, he will be a perfect conformist. If he absolutizes his personal identity he will risk to become indeterminate, to loose any communication with the other members of his society. In both these cases the individual has no power. Power appears thus connected to the capacity to deal with the contradictory requirements of the relationship between determinacy (social identity) and indeterminacy (personal identity).

1.2 The extrinsic power the individual

Also extrinsic power is a capacity to deal with the contradictory nature of social situation, but in this case such capacity does not develop within the subject himself, but at the level of social relations, where it does not matter that it be a *real* capacity but that it be a capacity *attributed* to the social actor. Therefore intrinsic and extrinsic power do not necessarily coincide in the same individual.

The attribution of extrinsic power to a subject can be caused due to diverse reasons, both from the point of view of the internal or external qualities of the subject to whom power is attributed (aggressiveness, narcissism, physical strength, energy, intelligence, skill, etc.) and from the point of view of the motivations which belong to the subjects who attribute power. There are two crucial elements in the latter: the first *subjective*, refers to the tendency of loading the other with the weight of risks and responsibility connected to the intrinsic or extrinsic exercise of power; the second, *objective*, is connected to the specific function which power assumes in a social context, as reduction of complexity and mean of communication (cfr. Luhman, 1975). From this point of view, in fact power seems to be a fundamental dimension of social order, strictly linked to the functioning of symbolic-normative forms of mediation.

As a matter of fact, a normative mediation requires first a "legislator" able to translate into synthetic norms the complex necessities of social life and then an "executive power" to implement them. A norm can really function only if founded on the determinacy which, as we have seen, is at the basis of predictability (certainty of the law) and on the norm's adaptation to reality (interpretation of the norm). It is also necessary that observance of the norms should be controlled (judicial function). But social life is not just application of norms, it is also experience, capacity of facing events, project, all dimensions which demand decision.

To adapt norms means to relativize them, to endanger their strength related to absolutization. Power, as the capacity of managing the relation between determinacy and indeterminacy, is the function which maintains normative order, while relativizing the norms. The attribution of power allows in fact the subject to establish absolute norms *for the others*, while the subject to whom power is attributed does not have to observe them in the same way. Power as such enjoys some discretion: it allows the transgression of norms without jeopardizing the normative order, it allows the continuity of the social order while transforming rules. Without power the function of symbolic mediation forms would be suffocated by their own absolutization: when these forms become crystalized, they are not useful any more, because they cannot really mediate experience.

In order to manage social contingencies the function of power is thus an essential machanism which reduces complexity, maintains the adaptability of the system and saves energies spent in maintaining consensus and coordinating actions. In this perspective, power is a reassurance towards predictability as well as a major source of unpredictability: hence the both protective and threatening nature of power.

In some mythological representations of power and political theories have been underscored these peculiar and ambivalent attributes of power; the double character of the man of power who is at the same time a legislator and a transgressor.

For instance, Moses in the Old Testament offers a good example of the different characteristics of power: the man of power who takes risks in relation with indeterminacy (Moses goes to the Sinai to talk with God); the man of power as legislator (Moses comes down with the laws); the man of power as transgressor (Moses breaks the stones on which the God's laws were written cfr. Crespi, 1982, 136).

The double characteristics of the man of power as representative and transgressor of laws is adumbrated also in the rituals for the coronation of a new king in some primitive societies. Such rituals rule that the future king must perform a series of symbolic or real transgressions of the most sacred laws (from sexual taboos to forcible seigure of property) so that he appears as the "transgressor *par excellence*" (Girard, 1972, 143).

Among theorists of power, besides Machiavelli, who understood the function of the prince as simulator and dissimulator, many authors from Bodin to Hobbes and to Carl Schmitt stressed the dimension of decision. Schmitt defined power as "decision in the case of exception" (Schmitt, 1922, 44 ff). In the exceptional situation normative forms do not provide enough information about correct behaviour and therefore a capacity of decision going beyond the norms is necessary (Schmitt, ibidem, 36 ff.)

Even Weber, stressing the *charismatic* characteristic of power and the *heroic* characteristic of the leader and distinguishing between ethic of conviction and ethic of responsibility highlighted this dimension of power (Weber, 1922).

The characters of law breaking and of decision, as crucial components of power in its relation with the symbolic-normative forms of mediation, allows the understanding of the difference between the *influence* of the man of faith and the *power* of the political leader. Who, like Christ, strongly *believes* in his truths and norms, he can obtain a large consensus among masses and influence their behaviour for many centuries, but he will not have any political power. Who on the contrary, *does not believe* (or at least believes with reservations) the certainties which he himself proclaims and uses unscrupulous ideology to be able to wield political power.

1.3 *Power as structure and function of the social system*

Power has to be studied not only as an intrinsic or extrinsic quality of the social actor, but also as an essential dimension of the social system. The general definition of power as the capacity to deal with the contradictions of the relationship between determinacy and indeterminacy applies also to power as a structure and function. Power's function is in fact very closely connected to the capacity of building respect to collective norms without considering them as absolute. A function to adapt the normative order to the changing and umpredictable contingencies of the relations between social system and its environment.

From a structural point of view power appears thus as an internal regulatory mechanism of the social system itself, connected to its material, organizational and institutional dimensions. At this level power is more than anything else a *position* a *status-role* which, within the social organization, defines the power of the subject, fixing the limits of his actions and responsibilities. Every social institution, as a determinate set of normative forms of symbolic mediation, defining the ways power may be exercised and the objective and subjective prerequisites of its attribution, establishes the functions which will permit the institution itself to act and to assure its adaptation and its goals attainment.

In the institutionalised system, power can be considered as the specific code which regulates the relation between the determinate forms of normative mediation and the indeterminate dimensions of social action. Mediation, as we have seen tends to fall into total absolutization so losing its capacity to mediate experience. In order to avoid this it needs a mechanism working against crystallization. This mechanism is precisely what we call here structural power, that is to say a set of rules establishing how and when power must be exercised (formal power). The managing of the relation between determinacy and indeterminacy, which at first we have analysed as a subjective capacity, appears now objectified in the same forms of symbolic mediation.

The structural dimension of power however is not only connected to the transfer of the function of power to a normative codified order establishing in what conditions power can be attributed and the ways it can be exercised, but it is also related to the distribution of economic resources and the different institutional structures.

The structure of power as the product of codified social actions is generally analysed in terms of inequality and class structure.

The analysis of the nature of symbolic mediation, in its connection with social action and power, shows that social inequality is not only connected to economic factors or to differences in the capacities of social actors, but it is also the consequence of the reductive character of symbolic mediation itself. Determinacy, as we have said above, is always constituted through the selection of some possibilities of action and the negation of all the other (see Luhmann, 1971). The social identities of the social actors and the roles attributed to them in the social system are a result of such a determination process But, as we have seen, the social identity of the individual does not necessarily coincide with his personal identity. In the particularity of their individual relations with others and with the environment, subjects can derive other forms of symbolic mediation in order to build a personal identity different from the one attributed to them by the social system. Individuals, groups, classes can thus develop relatively autonomous identities, differentiated from or even opposed to the prevailing system, which eventually can become their dominant social identities. The fact that social actors' experience can create differentiations into the degree of correspondence between the codified system of social identities and roles and the particular forms of identity elaborated by individuals, groups, classes, explains the differentiations along the axis from central to marginal positions within the social system itself.

The origin of inequality is therefore, in the last analysis, cennected to the reductive character of any determinate forms of symbolic-normative mediation: no symbolic order will be never able to correspond in the same way to the different needs and requests of all the members of a society. This shows that inequality cannot be totally eliminated and stresses another aspect of the conflictual character of social situation. If individuals would coincide perfectly with their social identities, the problem of inequality would not exist, since there would be only objective differences. Identified to these differences everyone would feel perfectly realised, as we see it happens in animal societies, characterised by the full correspondence between each individual and its "social" function. But human subjects are from the beginning in an ambivalent position toward identity and for this reason they will always suffer from the inequality of correspondence between the opportunities offered by the prevailing system of symbolic mediations and their own personal desires and needs.

2. *The dynamics of power*

Extrinsic power and structural power can be seen as two different aspects of the function of normative regulation and adaptation of social systems. As far as the system can deal with the contradictions arising within itself or coming from the outside and keeps adapting to new conditions or integrating new elements, we can say that the system has a certain *stability*. A stability which could be understood as "order through fluctuations" (see Prigogine-Stengers, 1979,174 ff.), since it is based on the degree of flexibility reached by the system in managing the determinacy relation. In this case the social system can include a plurality of forms of symbolic mediation and of sub-systems. These may be totally or partly contrasting with the prevailing order, without really threatening its capacity of self-regulation. When instead internal conflicts or external pressures cause tensions which the system cannot control, then the system gets into a state of *crisis*, due to the gap between the institutional dimensions of the system and the real forms of social action. If the system reaches a *critical point* from which it is impossible to revert to the previous state, a *catastrophe* or irreversible break of the system's structural stability can occur (see Thom, 1972), causing indeterminacy or anomie. In this case an excess of complexity is produced, which will have to be dealt with through new forms of reductive mediations. This latter will as well produce sooner or later unwanted effects and contradictions which will lead the system to a new critical point and so on, without ever reaching a final solution.

Obviously the degree of flexibility of social systems varies along a continuum from *rigid* and *closed* systems to *flexible* and *open* systems.

The rigid system is characterized by the predominance of functions oriented to maintaining stability and control against changes and by closure of outside stimuli. In such systems the degree to which the forms of symbolic-normative mediation are made absolute seems maximum; the values of consensus are exalted while power is considered the expression of such a consensus and by this coercion tends to be concealed.

This system considers contradictions, conflicts, and forms of deviance as pathological elements to be controlled and eliminated as transitory imperfections of a level of integration not yet fully achieved. Such system therefore tends to consider structures as valid and indisputable, without recognizing in them also a cause of contradictions, conflicts, anomie, and deviance which are attributed instead to the irrational character of the social actors and the deficiencies in their imperfect socialization. Hence in such conditions the social texture is considered as homogeneous and no differentiations are recognized if not linked to codified social functions and roles.

It is necessary however to observe that the abstract ideal of the rigid and closed system is not real: this pure type could never exist, because of its excessive degree of absolutization, it could not perform its functions in relation with the changing exigencies of experience. "Rigid and closed" systems actually function in history only thanks to the gap between their official forms and the effective inter-relational dynamics which go over and through institutional structures, particularly at the level of the ruling classes. The power of these latter finds its legitimacy in the management of systemic contradictions precisely because it never adheres too rigidly to the absolutized symbolic-normative forms, which are affirmed in principle but not respected in practice. Even in the most rigid systems there is always a certain degree of flexibility, although tensions, conflicts, contradictions, and deviance are kept latent. The weakness of the "rigid" system consists in the fact that they cannot institutionalize conflicts formally, regulating them explicitly, and therefore they risk the unpredictability of long repressed and uncontrolled indeterminacy. This type of system is forced to strengthen its internal cohesion, stressing continuously the threats which can come from without, either as economic competition or ideological attack, or as a war. All this makes gradual adaptation very difficult in rigid systems and sometimes even minimal transformations can lead such systems to critical and irreversible points.

Opposed to the rigid and closed system, historically represented for example by the totalitarian Soviet regime, is the ideal type of the "flexible and open" system. In this last one contradictions, tensions, conflicts are recognized as potentially induced by the social structures themselves and therefore as normal elements to be controlled through differentiated symbolic mediation and the institutionalization of communications which express self-criticism. Conflicts can be expressed without threatening the entire system and can promote eventual reform and adaptation. Structuring and destabilizing processes constitute normal functioning and their acknowledgment guarantees the system a dynamic equilibrium. In this context, deviance, either as symptom or as active opposition to the prevailing order, is considered to be a factor of the system's transformation, flexible and open structure allows the social system to maintain continuous exchanges with the outside and recognize internally the actual or potential heterogeneity of social forces. It is a pluralist, articulated and differentiated system not only in terms of its division of labour and roles, but also in diverse expressive forms of collective and individual subjectivity. In these systems power is recognized not only as a product of consensus, but also as having a coercive dimension, a minor evil to be avoided and controlled through the division of powers and a continuous vigilance against its concentration tendencies.

Like "rigid" systems the ideal type of the "flexible and open" system is never totally realized in practice. Difficulties in managing the relation determinacy-indeterminacy witness the fluctuation of flexible systems on one side toward absolutization to the point of compromising their ability to adapt, and on the other side toward an excess of indeterminacy which could lead to catastrophic fall either into a rigid system or into dissolution of any social order. Even in the context of flexible systems the exceptional character of power's decision and the function of power's "unscrupulousness" are clear. The "flexible" system functions often because power does not observe in practice the principles of pluralism and openness officially affirmed. If the force of the open system is its flexibility and the manifest character of its conflicts, its weakness is represented by the danger of too much complexity and, consequently by its incapacity of providing those conditions of certainty and reassurance which are generally required by the majority of the social actors who lack intrinsic power. An efficient political power will take care of these aspects, even if it will have to go against some democratic rules. Here too the ambivalence of power appears as a quality essential to its function.

In some respects the Anglo-Saxon type of democratic regime corresponds to the flexible and open system. Between the two extreme models here considered, which can be applied either to national social systems or to internal sub-systems, there are the diverse "mixed" forms of concrete social systems, whose specific characters and particular conditions must be verified empirically in their historical situations.

In such diverse systems the deep causes behind fast and radical changes can be singled out first as the outcomes of tensions and conflicts produced by the reduction of complexity in any established order; second, by the incapacity of the system's subjects to manage the contradictions due either to absolutization and consequent crystalization of established orders or to the weakening of the symbolic-normative forms of mediation which produce too much indeterminacy and insecurity in social life. In reality the two contrapposed alternatives are often linked to each other, since tensions and conflicts threatening the order tend to cause stiffening of power, which will seek to bolster itself either through a further absolutization of legitimizing forms of mediation, or through resorting to the pure indeterminacy of its own absolute will.

In the first case, the more power trusts the forms of legitimacy, the more it risks losing its specific function of founding and guaranteeing normative orders while assuming the responsibility of exceptional decisions. In the second case, if power becomes a form of decision independent from legitimizing norms and consensus, it risks losing legitimacy the more it appears to be coercive.

Both cases can be considered as outcomes of an incapacity of managing the relation determinacy-indeterminacy, which leads power to a dead end. Strengthening power requires absolutizing institutional arrangements, but such absolutization stresses the gap between institutions and reality. This situation stresses the decisional and coercive nature of power in the face of new social demands, but thus it also contributes to undermining traditional legitimacy, opening the way to new subjects of power.

If the objective weakening of the capacity for managing of the established power can appear as one of the necessary conditions to the revolutionary explosion, this however is not a sufficient cause. Not always an excessively rigid power in its formalistic positions (absolutization of the legitimate institutional forms) or a power which appears in its coercive character are displaced by revolutionary upheavals. Revolution itself is a very rare event, most of all if we consider the historical phenomena without resorting to ideology. Most of the time a ruling class incapable of managing contradictions is integrated with new elements of other classes and can therefore be substituted gradually, with some violent episodes, but without global transformation of the system. Even in the case of revolutions (English revolution of 1688, French revolution in 1789, Chinese in 1911, etc.) the social system is never totally renovated: often the bureaucratic-administrative structures of the State survive in spite of changes in the ruling political class, of transformations of the political constitutional forms or of the relations of power between classes.

Even in this case the essential function of power is confirmed, as well as the fact that power survives only owing to its capacity for managing emergent contradictions in reality, guaranteeing the essential conditions of predictability and adaptation through reduction of complexity even at the expense of relative incoherence with regards to the legitimizing forms of symbolic mediation.

3. *A perspective of emancipation*

The analysis of power shows, as we have seen, the intimate connection between the ambivalence of power and the contradictions of social situation. A non-utopian perspective of collective emancipation should start precisely from the consideration of that ambivalence and those contradictions, leaving aside the dream of a final and total overcoming of the last ones in a perfect society free from conflicts and differentiations.

Bertrand de Jouvenel affirms that in every society there are individuals who do not feel protected enough the "security seeking" and individuals who do not feel free enough the "libertarians" (cfr. de Jouvenel, 1947, 414). If it is true that in reality there are individuals disposed to risk, fighting for freedom, and others who manifest the need for reassurance, both tendencies are potentially present in every social subject, as he is caught in the oscillation of the determinacy—indeterminacy relation. From the subject's point of view therefore the problem of emancipation, (increased autonomy and a greater critical responsibility with regards to the social order and the structure of domination) presents itself in the terms of strengthening one's capacity for taking the risk inherent in such a relation. Only through an increased faculty for managing the contradictions of the existential situation can there be a radical change in the relations of power. It is in fact necessary to break the simple alternation between pushes towards anarchy or totalitarian authoritarianism, which is the consequence of the masses lack of intrinsic power and of their illusory search for definitive resolution of contradictions.

If effective vital exigencies of renovation or stability are both essential to the social order, and manifest themselves in the tendencies both of a "libertarian" or "security seeking" type, they also express a fundamental inadequacy in managing the unstable equilibrium of the social order, an inadequacy which is a source of more or less grave social destructiveness.

As we have seen, power itself does not always keep up with its function and trends, therefore, to remain caught in the vicious circle between the tendency towards determinacy, through an absolutization of the legitimizing institutional forms, or that towards the indeterminacy of its absolute will. The re-establishment of the power's function after its deterioration through the substitution of one power elite with another will not be immune from dangers of involution. The conflictual alternation between diverse forms of power cannot therefore be seen as a dialectic progress, but as the result of an oscillation linked to processes of adaptation in a situation which as such is not solvable once for all.

The problem of the ideal conditions which, on the level of cultural and social formation of the individual can favour an emancipatory project, is extremely complex and cannot be put forward here in all its dimensions.

I will just point to a particularly difficult aspect about the theoretical perspective of emancipation. As I have said, on one hand the identity of social actors is strictly dependent on the forms of social determinacy and shows the need for symbolic orders of representations, and for relatively coherent, consistent norms. On the other hand, the limit of determinacy linked to the fatally reductive character of mediating forms underscores also the subject's need to achieve a relative autonomy from the more codified forms of social identity. The possibility of offering a more adequate space to the emerging subjectivity on its own terms seem to lay not on the reconstitution of 'strong' models of identity as in the bourgeois tradition, but on a social "unconditional" recognition of the subject's *being* previous to every demand to adapt to the codified forms of social predictability (role, function, etc.) The foundation of sociability should not be based on the principle: "I recognize your being only *if* you adapt to the expected norms," but on the reverse one: "since I entirely recognize you in your unobjectifiable being, I invite you to adapt to the norms in order to constitute together a social order."

At a pedagogical level the ideal model of the non-possessive love, that is to say the capacity to recognize the difference of the other in its infinite character, remains the most elevated model for a gratuitous confirmation of the other's being (Levinas, 1974). At a sociological level the same model could be translated in the collective forms of ritual and of juridical-institutional type, in order to recognize identity and social appurtenance as primary conditions of every other form of social participation. In such cases the confirmation of the identity would not hide the dimension of difference, from which all the possibilities and the power itself of the subject develop.

It is here that a theoretical and practical difficulty shows up. As I said, the increase in the subject's intrinsic power toward his emancipation appears linked to the subject's possibility for recognizing the limits and reductive character of social orders and of each form of constitutive symbolic mediation.

This recognition however is working against an essential condition at the basis of social predictability: that degree of absolutization without which no determinacy can exist. In these terms the ideal of emancipation seems to contrast with the conditions of sociability. If the increase in the intrinsic power implies the weakening of social rules, through the recognition of their conventional character, it becomes hard to generalize that increase since one should suppose at the beginning an equal capacity on the part of every member of society for managing the relation determinacy-indeterminacy. This condition appears utopian not only because historically the recognition of radical conventionality meets with great resistances provoking existential anxieties which favour regression towards absolute orders, but because, even if we hypothesize a society of *mature* adults, there will be always the problem of infants and adolescents for whom the impossibility of every 'certain' reference would have a destructive result. This consideration shows the inconsistency of an ideal model of society without differentiation between those who know and those who do not know, between the consciousness of those who rule and those who do not rule, between those who have the capacity of relativizing and those who feel the need for absolutization. Even under this respect the project of a total elimination of power appears unreal.

The perspective of a universal emancipation, next to the tragic, irresolvable character of the social situation, seems to give way to a more pragmatic attitude which looks for partial forms of unstable equilibrium and for limitation of the absolute tendencies present either in the nature of symbolic mediation or in the dynamic of domination. Although one must accept the inevitability of inequality in different subjects intrinsic power and therefore, in some way, cannot disregarded completely enlightened or elitist attitudes, one can always tend to democratic forms of society, as "open" social systems with flexible structures in which absolutization is reserved only to certain values and certain fundamental rules of living, allowing the greatest possible degree of pluralism of choices. But even in this case we cannot forget that there is no dimension guaranteeing a full immunity from the risks of domination (cfr. Crespi, 1983. 254 ff.)

If, however, the contradictions present in the social world have their common root in the contradictory character of the existential situation, the lack of a solution to such a situation at the social level is not of the same character as that present at the level of individual experience. The constitutive limit of the respect for the presence of all in the social context, from which the necessity of "standard" forms of symbolic-normative mediation derives, is not the same limit of the personal experience which can go beyond social boundaries. With this I do not want to mean that the subject can realize itself without society, as the depth of his existential experience is, in the last analysis, linked to the way he succeeds to integrated in his life the cultural and social components which are constitutive of his self. But the experience of negative transcendence of consciousness is a dimension which escapes the social horizon, even though it is always active within it. From such dimension the intrinsic power of the subject derives its possibility to appear as an essential, if not sufficient, condition to introduce in society a dimension of authentic change.

REFERENCES

Crespi, F. (1982) *Mediazione simbolica e societa*, Milano, F. Angeli.

———(1983) *Assenza di fondamento e progetto sociale* in G. Vattimo—P.A. Rovatti (a cura di) *It pensiero debole*, Milano, Feltrinelli.

——(1985) *Le vie della sociologia*, Bologna, Il Mulino.

De Jouvenel, B. (1947) *Du Pouvoir*, Geneve, Bourquin.

Girard, R. (1972) *La violence et le sacre*, Paris, Grasset.

Goffman, E. (1959) *Presentation of Self in Everyday Life*, New York, Doubleday.

———(1961) *Encounters: Two Studies in the Sociology of Interaction* Indianapolis, Bobbs Merril.

Levinas, E. (1974) *Totalite et Infini*, La Haye, M. Nijhoff.

Luhmann, N. (1971) *Politische Planning*, Opladen, Westdeutscher Verlag.

———(1975) *Macht*, Stuttgart, Ferdinand Enke.

Manciulli, M.et al. (1986) *Il dilemma organizzativo*, Milano, F. Angeli.

Prigogine, I.—Stengers I. (1979) *La Nouvelle Alliance*, Paris, Gallimard.

Schmitt, C. (1922) *Politische Theologie, Vier Kapitel zur Lehre der Souveranitat* Munchen-Leipzig, Duncker-Humblot.

Thom, R. (1972) *Stabilite structurelle et morphogenese*, Paris, Inter-Editions.

Turner, R. (1968) *The Self-Conception in Social Interaction* in Gordon C.—Gergen K. (eds.) *The Self in Social Interaction*, New York, Wiley.

Weber, M. (1922) *Wirtschaft und Gesellschaft*, Tubingen, Mohr.

2

SCIENCE VALUES AND DEMOCRATIC THEORY

PETER RONALD DE SOUZA*

I wish to draw attention to an important issue that emerged in the debate of the 50's and 60's in political theory, that of the relationship between science, values and democratic theory. I have chosen to examine this relationship because I consider it to be at the centre of the major controversy on the possibility of a participatory democracy, and also because I recognize that some confusion persists on the nature of the relationship between the normative and empirical dimensions of political theory. I have located my discussion in the realm of democratic theory because it is here where this relationship can be most effectively illustrated by the arguments between the realistic/

*I wish to thank Prof. T.B. Bottomore for his support and very useful comments on an earlier version of this draft, and to Ralph Bannell, Paul Fox-Strangways, and Ligia Noronha for their constructive criticisms. However, I alone am responsible for any inadequacies in argument, for notpaying due attention to the 'inconvenient facts' they pointed out. I am also grateful to the International Sociological Association, the British Sociological Association, and the University of Sussex for enabling me to attend the XIth would congress of International Sociological Association held in Delhi in August 1986.

empirical theorists of democracy and their opponents, the neo-classical theorists of democracy.

The realistic theorists were dissatisfied with what they considered to be the 'classical theory of democracy', with the unrealistic scenarios described and justified by these 'classical' theorists. They felt that the central concepts used by such theorists, concepts suchas 'common good', 'general will', 'rational citizen', etc., had no basis in fact, and were therefore utopian impositions upon the actual sociological processes of politics. In opposition to the ideas of Rousseau, Bentham, the two mills, (James Mill and J.S. Mill) Tocqueville, and possibly even Marx, the realistic theorists attempted to develop a realistic, value-free, conception of democracy based on the results of their detailed empirical studies.

Weber and Michels were among the first to level this charge of the lack of realism in the classical discussions of democracy. It was most systematically addressed, however, by Schumpeter in his monumental and influential work *Capitalism Socialism and Democracy*' (1942). The attempt by these realistic/empirical theorists was to re-define democracy by challenging its central conceptions, in particular the concept of the rational, self-conscious citizen who in an unconstrained society would be able to realize his/her capacities, potential, powers or utilities. The two groups to which these theorists belong can be classified as the 'weak' empirical group which includes theorists such as Weber, Schumpeter, and G. Sartori, and the 'strong' empirical group which includes theorists such as B. Berelson, P. Lazarsfeld, H.D. Lasswell, D. Easton, R.A. Dahl, and S.M. Lipset. The difference between them lies in their attitude to the role of ultimate values in social theory, especially in political theory.[1] The former group attempted to minimize the influence of values in political analysis while recognizing that some influence will always be there, the attempt being to increase the aspect of intersubjectivity, whereas the latter group, influenced by a particular interpretation of positivism, attempted to develop a scientific politics.[2]

The neo-classical response to this attempt by the realistic theorists was guided by two factors. The first, and chronologically earlier factor, was the need in the 50's and the 60's to defend political philosophy against the onslaught of political science. To this factor can be attributed the articlse by G. Duncan and S. Lukes, L. Davis, I. Berlin, C. Taylor and J.L. Walker.[3] The second was the need to explain the threat to the equilibrium and stability of the system posed by the student unrest, the civil rights movement, and the anti-Vietnam war domonstrations of the late sixties which were a direct challenge to the realistic theorists' arguments on consensus and apathy. Some of the writings of T.B. Bottomore, S. Bowles, C. Pateman P. Bachrach and M.S. Baratz can be understood in this perspective.[4] I cannot here trace the arguments of the different groups npr engage in a discussion of what each theorist said, or meant to say, or implied by saying, since such an endeavour would be beyond the par meters of my paper. I Shall focus instead on one aspect of their debate which illustrates their differing attitudes to the link between the normative and the empirical components of democracy, the aspect of the relationship between science, values, and democratic theory.

The attempt by the realistic theorists to construct an empirical theory of democracy should be seen as part of a larger movement to create a science of politics. This movement, enamoured of the progress of the physical sciences, and of the efficacy of their methods, aimed to adopt and adapt some of the tools and techniques of investigation developed by these sciences for the investigation of human societies. It attempted to generate factual information about how human beings order their lives, relate to each other, act, work, learn, and govern; and more generally, information about how they perform the whole range of activities that are the hallmark of human societies. The 'behavioural movement', as it came to be known, attempted to construct a systematic body of information on human behaviour which would measure up to the standards of accuracy, predictability, verifiability, and generalizability, that its proponents considered to be typical of the physical sciences, These studies raised important questions that needed to be addressed by theorists of politics. Are political philosophy and political science mutually exclusive, or are they bound together in a symbiotic relationship? How does the vast amount of data on politics generated by empirical investigation affect the propositions of political philosophy? Is a science of politics at all possible? Such questions increasingly came to be asked by political scientists who had come under the influence of the positivist tradition.

This call to emulate the physical sciences found early expression in the advice that Charles E. Merriam gave to the association of American political scientists. Inspired by the works of Arthur Bentley on pressure groups he too sought new techniques of investigation and new units of political analysis because, like them, he too was impatient with the formal approach in traditional political theory. In his presidential address of 1925 to the 'American Political Science Association' he advocated a scientific investigation of political behaviour, advice which was to serve as the basis of a plethora of studies on political behaviour later on.

> Some day we may take another angle of approach *than the formal, as other sciences do*, and begin to look at *political behaviour* as one of the essential objects of inquiry.[5]

Under Merriam's guidance, a tradition of empirical political studies developed at the University of Chicago. Involved in these investigations were Harold Lasswell, a faculty member, V.D. Key Jr., David Truman, Herbert Simon, and Gabriel Almond, who were graduate students in the department, and all of whom were actively engaged in constructing an empirical theory of democracy. This movement gained a fresh impetus from the influx into the US in the 1930's of European scholars such as Franz Neumann, Paul Lazarsfeld, Hans Gerth, and Reinhard Bendix, who brought with them 'a sociological approach to politics that strongly reflected the specific influence of Max Weber.[6] Weber's methodological arguments, especially those relating to objectivity in the social sciences, hence came to exert a considerable influence on political research, particularly since many of the above-mentioned scholars later occupied important positions in the American academic system.

Political behaviour as an area of research found ready appeal, since it lent itself easily to empirical investigation, especially in the field of voting. A vast literature on electoral behaviour thus developed as a consequence of the behavioural movement in politics.[7] It furnished a 'realistic' picture of how the political subject chooses between competing options, assesses claims, expresses preferences, indicates interest, and more generally comprehends the processes of politics. These valuable sociological insights into the ways in which the voter participates and responds to the political process, reinforced the demand for a revision of the presuppositions of traditional theory and for the establishment of a new foundation for political theory.[8] Classical theories of democracy were the most vulnerable to these data on elections, especially since they were premised on the conception of a rational moral being who had certain inalienable fundamental rights, or had certain inherent capacities which needed to be realized, as has been argued by the 'negative' and 'positive' liberty traditions respectively. Democracy was seen by both negative and positive libertarians as the best means for the attainment of freedom, since it embodied certain principles, was organized around certain procedures, and promoted certain processes of politics of which the opportunity to participate was considered as one of the most valuable.

This theme of participation in politics, divided contemporary theorists of democracy into two traditions, the realistic and the neo-classical traditions, the former aiming to construct an empirical theory of democracy based on their reading of what was required by a positivist conception of science, and the latter arguing on normative grounds against the feasibility of such an exercise.[9] In this paper I do not intend merely to assess the merits and inadequacies of the arguments on participatory democracy,[10] but to extend the discussions developed so far into an area that involves both normative and empirical issues, especially since inadequate attention has been given to the relationship between science and values in democratic theory. This is particularly glaring since the major point of contention implicit in the two traditions has been the fact that, on the one hand, classical political philosophers have been accused by the realistic theorists of not paying much attention to the issue of the empirical adequacy of their moral propositions while, on the other empirical theorists have been charged with crroneously assuming, in their eagerness to provide a 'realistic' account of democracy, that the only way to do so was through a 'value-free' approach.

These disputes on a science of politics, and on an empirical theory of democracy, are put into perspective when viewed within the context described by the following three questions: (i) What is the significance of the central conception of political philosophy, which is that of the individual as a morally autonomous person, for democratic theory? (ii) How is democracy as a 'means' to an end, and as an 'end in itself,' related to this central conception? and, (iii) How do the empirical findings of sociology affect the conception of democracy as a means and as an end? The first two questions are ignored by the realistic theorists, and the third is overlooked by the neo-classical theorists, as the following excerpts from their discussions indicate.

Pateman merely states that, as Duncan and Lukes point out, empirical evidence can lead us to change normative theories under certain circumstances, although they add that as far as changing the ideal is concerned "it needs to be shown exactly how and why the ideal is rendered improbable or impossible of attainment."[11] Duncan and Lukes recognize the problem and argue that the proof of the lack of realism of 'classical' theory, can only 'be really convincing if one could show that traditional democratic theory made demands which men are by nature unable to satisfy. Only then would the ideal be literally *invalidated*, for it would have been shown that the obstacles to its realization are irremovable . . . only then could the facts (about human nature) even in principle serve to invalidate the old theories of domocracy.[12] Duncan and Lukes base their discussion of this relationship between science and values on Runciman who, in turn, bases his discussion on Max Weber.[13] The issue of the 'naturalistic fallacy' that has engaged moral philosophers is not addressed, and this is a major omission especially since the issue of the logical relationship between 'is' and 'ought' statements and the relationship between 'fact' and 'value' hovers menacingly in the background. The fact that both the behaviouralist movement and their critics ultimately seem to draw inspiration from the same methodological discussions of Max Weber, exemplifies once again the lack of clarity in the discussions in democratic theory on the relationship between science and values. And yet, it is a relationship that cannot be wished away.

Another factor that contributed to this confusion is the ambiguity in the use of the term 'democratic theory' in the vast literature on democratic politics. This is an ambiguity that has been carried over from the use of the term 'political theory' which refers to discussions both in political philosophy and political science. The confusion arises because of the elastic use of the word 'theory' which refers to both descriptions and frameworks of explanation. A description need not establish causal relations, whereas an explanation must do so. This it does by reference to a set of interrelated general principles which, as Taylor states, delineates 'the important dimensions of variation for the range of phenomena concerned.'[14] In a social theory these principles are both normative and empirical in nature.

A democratic theory is, therefore, a set of interrelated general principles relating to the nature and features of democratic processes and society. It contains two component parts, a specification of means and a specification of ends. A democracy will be regarded as a configuration of political institutions which enable 'the people' to govern themselves. These institutions will be seen as organized around principles which encourage the broadest involvement of the majority of citizens in the formulation and implementation of, and participation in, those political decisions and activities that are matters concerning, and have an effect upon, the whole collectivity.

Three separate aspects of relevance for this study are subsumed by this relationship between science and values. They are the relationship between: (i) political philosophy and democratic theory, (ii) political philosophy and political science and (iii) democratic theory and political science. The separation into these three aspects is made here merely as an analytical technique to emphasize certain features, though I recognize that such a distinction does not exist in the literature since there is a considerable degree of overlap between each of these different aspects. To illustrate better the relationship between science, values, and democratic theory, I find it useful to recognize that the various themes under discussion in the recent literature on democracy may be brought under four headings: the *meaning* of democracy, the *conditions* of democracy, the *justification* of democracy, and the *relation of democracy to other political concepts and principles.*[15]

These discussions also involve formal, normative, and empirical issues. (i) They are of a formal character when the etymological roots of the words are examined, the logical consistency of arguments assessed, the implications of concepts discussed, and the dependence and relationship between concepts identified. (ii) They are of a normative character when the value basis of political activity and political institutions is stated. This value basis is of a primary type when democracy is seen as an end-in-itself (*e.g.*, equals should be treated equally), and is of a secondary type when it is seen as a means for the furtherance of other ends (*e.g.*, liberty). And finally, (iii) they are of an empirical nature when the sociological linkages between the different aspects of democratic politics are examined, and the mechanisms of 'who gets what, when, and how' are investigated. These distinctions will be better shown by the following discussion which examines the main links between political philosophy, political science, and democratic theory.

To put it briefly the basic concern of political philosophy is with identifying, examining, and justifying a set of desirable ends as features of the 'good society.' Particular forms of authority are considered to be consistent with these features, and these forms of authority are prescribed by the various theorists since they promote desirable ends. The discussions in political philosophy therefore consist of varied responses to the question 'why should anyone obey anyone else?', the variety of answers being due mainly to the fact that no consensus exists on what is an acceptable form of political authority consistent with the 'good society', and hence, by extension, no consensus on what are the acceptable justifications for political obedience and obligation. Notions such as sovereignty, liberty, equality, justice, etc., and the relationship between them, come into play. The history of political thought bears witness to these inconclusive disputes on desirable ends and in a sense is illustrative of Berlin's flourish when he says: 'If we ask the Kantian question. "In what kind of world is political philosophy—the kind of discussion and argument in which it consists—in principle possible?" the answer must be 'only in a world where ends collide.'[16]

Underlying many of these discussions were diverse conceptions of human nature. Different political philosophers considered different attributes as essential to the human beings and hence ideal societies had to be conceptualised in such a way that these attributes would find full expression. Various scenarios were imagined by the 'classical' theorists, scenar os which allowed them to state their view of what was essential to human nature, an essence which had thus to be either protected or promoted by the duly constituted political authority. Hobbes, Locke, and Rousseau in the 17th and 18th centuries and even Rawls in the 20th century, resorted to such devices as the 'state of nature' or 'the social contract' to establish their case for what they considered to be the fundamental basis of the relationship between the individual and society. Popular notions like liberty, equality, justice, the pursuit of happiness, etc., were involved in the discussions of this ideal relationship which was regarded as the fullest expression of the 'good society.' The literature on the substantive features of each of these ends, and on the relationship between them, is very extensive and it will be possible here to discuss briefly only one of them in order to highlight the relationship between political philosophy and democratic theory. The discussion on liberty has been chosen as particularly illuminating.

Discussions in political philosophy on the concept of democracy, were 'concerned with the achievement in society of what were regarded as various desirable human ends.'[17] Based on a certain conception of human nature, they examined the conditions required by the 'good society', conditions which were both normative and empirical. This examination of necessary conditions is effectively illustrated by the differing conceptions of liberty which have been grouped into 'negative' and 'positive' liberty traditions. The former conception emphasizes the inviolable area within which an individual or group of persons should be able 'to do or not do, to be or net to be, or to become or not to become something,' without external interference.[18] This is an argument not just for preserving the autonomy of the individual, but also for protecting the individual from the unjust actions of external authority. This minimum area where an individual is free from interference, free to do or be what he or she wishes to do or be, is regarded as integral to the human person, so that a violation of it would constitute a degradation of that which is essentially human.

> What then must this minimum be? That which a man cannot give up without offending against the essence of his nature. What is this essence? What are the standards which it entails? This has been, and perhaps will be, a matter of infinite debate But whatever the principle in terms of which the area of non-interference is to be drawn, whether it is that of natural law or natural rights, or of utility, or the pronouncements of a categorical imperative, or the sanctity of the social contract, or any other concept with which men have sought to clarify and justify their convictions, liberty in this sense means liberty *from*; absence of interference beyond the shifting, but always recognizable frontier.[19]

This condition of respect for an inviolable area is not a necessary minimum condition for democracy. In fact, the negative conception of liberty is not incompatible with autocracy, since the concern in this conception is primarily with the issue of non-interference by political authority in a minimal area, and not with the nature of political authority itself.[20] Hence it is possible to argue that if a benevolent dictator respects this minimal area, then his/her government can be said to ensure liberty. Democracy as a system of government is thus not a necessary consequence of a 'negative' conception of liberty. It is merely the best guarantor of such 'negative' liberty.

Contrasting with this the 'positive' conception of liberty is concerned with the nature of government, with the question 'who is to say what I am, and what I am not to be or do?[21] The realization of the human essence is of concern in this conception which seeks to establish the necessary and sufficient conditions for the expression of this human essence, defined in terms of human capacities, powers, potentials, or utilities.[22] 'Positive' freedom seeks to define the ideal relationship between the individual and society. It recognizes that only in such a relationship will the individual be able to exercise control over the direction of his/her own life. 'Positive' freedom is contingent upon the existence of certain social conditions which are considered necessary for self-realization.

It is believed that democracy creates some of these necessary conditions. In the case of positive liberty democracy provides the set of political iustitutions which promote this realization of human powers and capacities, since it gives the citizen an opportunity to participate, as the equal of other participants, in an important domain of social life, the realm of politics. It enables him/her to determine the norms that are to govern his/her social existence. It gives him/her a chance to promote his/her individual and collective interests, and therefore, democracy is considered as a means to an end. Political philosophy specifies the desirable ends which justify the processes and institutions of democracy and which provide the normative underpinning for characteistic features of democracy like accountability, separation of powers, responsibility, free and fair elections, etc., features that are regarded as indispensable to democratic government.

There is much disagreement among theorists about the composition of these integral features of government, because of the conflicting hierarchies of values and also because of their differing value-spheres such that what is considered as a vital and essential prerequisite from one viewpoint is considered as an irrelevant and dispensable feature from another. An example of this conflict of values is the issue of widespread political participation. On the one hand, it is considered as a threat to democracy by the realistic theorists who see it as leading to a destabilization of the political system, whereas, on the other hand, it is regarded by the neo-classical theorists as a fundamental feature of democracy since it promotes both self-protection and self-realization. This controversy can be further extended by looking at the findings of political science.

Answers to the question: What constitutes a 'realistic' explanation of political processes? Will demonstrate this link between political philosophy and political science. Though political philosophers were largely concerned with the normative issues of political authority, with why government ought to be obeyed, they also sought to explain how government functions or how it arose.'[23] For example, the notion of the 'common good' was developed to reconcile observable divergent interests in society, as a higher notion which suggested that there actually existed a homogeneity of interests for all members of a community. It was the validity of such notions as 'callective will', 'common good', 'rational behaviour' etc., which political science attempted to examine.

Using the techniques of investigation developed by the physical sciences, especially those developed by statistics, it became possible to collect and collate more reliable accurate information about the processes of politics. A detailed and thorough empirical investigation of politics thus became possible. The behaviour of citizens as legislators, administrators, or voters were studied, and this provided detailed insights into political behaviour such as apathy and devotion to a leader. It also provided information on the reasons why individuals participate, and on the extent of their knowledge on contemporary political issues. The notion of the rational, responsible citizen, a key notion in political philosophy, thus came to be challenged.

Some of these notions of political philosophy have both an empirical and a normative dimension, in that they make claims about the world and then use these claims to justify particular political configurations. These empirical claims, when subjected to logical scrutiny, are found to have the status of a minor premise which is linked to the particular ought-judgement, which is used to justify a particular political configuration, only because of the presence of a suppressed universal ought-principle. I shall illustrate this logical relationship when I come to discuss the question of the 'naturalistic fallacy.' It is these empirical claims that have been the cause of much dissatisfaction. The notion of the 'common good' is most telling. Empirical political studies showed that no homogeneity of interest existed in any political community, and therefore the argument that was advanced in favour of homogeneity was claimed by the realistic theorists to be inductive and unsupported by fact. This gulf between concept and fact led them to argue that only testable propositions of politics were to be considered valid. Since they regarded the propositions of political philosophy as being mainly normative and utopian, and so by their reasoning untestable, political philosophy was considered to be invalid, unrealistic and in need of revision. By empirical investigation political science was able to draw attention to the concepts of political philosophy and thereby to the normative dimension of politics. It therefore raised the issue that came to be a focal point of realistic studies, the issue of 'value-neutrality.' This is most clearly brought out in the debate on an empirical theory of democracy.

The detailed nature of empirical studies of elections yielded information about how individuals divided by sex, colour, kinship, caste, interest, race, age, religion, class, status, and income, participated in one of the more significant processes of democratic politice, *viz.*, the selection of representatives by vote. Various theses relating to participation were tested. Do people vote rationally? What is the degree of people's participation in the selection of representatives? What is the intensity of involvement in political issues? How do people ensure that representatives remain responsible to them? The empirical investigation of such questions brought into focus such notions of political philosophy as 'rule of the people', 'collective will', 'integrative function of participation', etc.[24]

> Although it is seldom made clear just which of the classical democratic theorists is being referred to, contemporary criticism has focussed primarily on the descriptive elements of the theory, on its basic conceptions of citizenship representation, and decision-making. The concept of an active, informed, democratic citizenry, the most distinctive feature of the traditional theory, is the principal object of attack. On empirical grounds it is argued that very few such people can be found in Western societies.[25]

The modified descriptive propositions of democratic theory that emerged as a result of such empirical investigation, however, still left the issue of value-neutrality unresolved. The argument that a theory of democracy must include empirical, value-neutral propositions, and that these propositions, must be testable, is not the same as the realistic theorists argument that a theory of democracy must consist only of such testable value-neutral propositions. Their argument that theories of democracy should be realistic and open to empirical investigation does not lead to the conclusion that there is no place for normative propositions in democratic theory. It is the confusion on this score that led the realistic theorists to advocate a democratic theory that is value-neutral. They had treated *normative as synonymous with utopian, and realistic as identical with value-neutral.*

This attempt to construct a value-neutral empirical theory of democracy was challenged successfully on two fronts. The first was based on the argument that all theories have a framework of delineation which gives the theory its organizing principle, the conceptual structure which helps it decide between more and less valid data. It gives the theory, as it were the geography of the range of phenomena in question, it tells us how they can vary, [and] what are the major dimensions of variation.[26] Since a social theory deals with the human situation, with human wants, needs and purposes, this framework of delineation consists of both normative and empirical principles. The notion of 'good' therefore cannot be excluded from such a theory since the satisfaction of human wants, needs and purposes' is *prima facie* considered to be 'good.' A democratic theory which consists of procedural rules, and justifications for these rules, relies on such a conception of 'good' to provide the needed justification. A democratic theory which consists of procedural rules, and justifications for these rules, relies on such a conception of 'good' to provide the needed justification. Thus the claim that the empirical theory of democracy is value-neutral is not tenable.

The second challenge comes from philosophers of language who argue that it is impossible to constitute the language of social theory with words and concepts that are purely descriptive.[27] Discussions of democracy involve conceptions of it as a 'means' for the achievement of a higher end, and also as an 'end in itself' and thus both normative and empirical issues are involved in democratic theory. The normative aspect demonstrates the logical link between conceptions of the good society (primary values) and conceptions of democracy. The empirical aspect shows the nature of democratic processes, the features of the procedures involved, and the functions of democratic structures as a means for the promotion of a higher end.

The preceding discussion has shown that notions of the 'good society' are not just fortuitously linked to democratic theory, but form an integral part of it in some cases explicitly stated, in others implicitly present; and they constitute the basis for the value-slope of democratic theory. On the basis of a brief content analysis of the different democratic theories, either those considered as normative, or those labelled as empirical, it can be shown that all consist of a minimum of the following three characteristics: (i) a notion of the 'good society' *i.e.*, either explicit or implicit and that is seen as the expression of the ideal relationship between the individual and society, (ii) at least one value-statement which is either a preference or a value-judgement, and (iii) at least one descriptive statement of an explanatory kind indicating causality.

The 'good society' is the expression of the ideal relationship between the individual and society and thus can be defined as one where all human beings are provided the opportunity to realize their powers, capabilities, or utilities. Normative propositions in democratic theory of the order. 'All members of a political community should have an equal right to participate in community affairs,' are derived from such a conception of the 'good society,' and hence statements of approval, preference, and commendation, are premised on it. Statements such as 'the liberty of individuals ought to be defended' or 'equals should be treated equally,' derive their justification from such a conception of the 'good society.' Those values which define the 'good society' will here be considered as primary values. Value statements which are of this order are not open to scientific proof or disproof, since science cannot indicate whether one set of primary values which defines the 'good society' is better than another.[28]

Value statements are of two kinds: (i) primary value-statements which are not open to scientific testing but are amenable to rational argument, in the sense that reasons which derive from the 'good society' have to be advanced for them, and (ii) secondary value-statements which are subject to scientific proof or disproof. Secondary value-statements are dependent on a factual assumption which makes such scientific testing possible.[29] They are thus of the order 'A ought to be done because B is the consequence. The issue of scientific testing raises the issue of the 'naturalistic fallacy' where one side in the debate has argued that there is no logical relationship between 'is' and 'ought' statements, *i.e.*, 'ought' cannot be derived from 'is', or 'ought' cannot be reduced to 'is', whereas the other side has claimed that the above is possible.[30]

The non-naturalists have argued that it is logically possible to move from a minor premise which is an 'is' statement to a conclusion which is a particular 'ought' judgement, only if there is a suppressed major premise which is a universal 'ought' principle. It will be useful here to cite an example from the democratic theory.

Minor premise (is—statement): Democracy is a system of government that ensures widespread political participation.

Conclusion (particular ought—judgement): Democracy ought to be desired.

The non-naturalists argue that the movement from the 'is' statement to the 'ought' judgement is logically possible only because of the suppressed major premise, the universal 'ought' principle which is the following.

Major premise (universal ought-principle): The system of government that promotes widespread political participation ought to be desired.

Further, through a process of logical analysis it can be shown that the above syllogism is linked to a preceding syllogism such that its universal 'ought' principle becomes the particular 'ought' judgement of the preceding syllogism. In this way it is possible to move through logical regress till ultimately one arrives at the notion of the 'good society.' The following example will illustrate this logical regress, by showing how the previous universal 'ought' principle, becomes a particular 'ought' judgement of the preceding syllogism.

Major premise (universal ought-principle): The system of government that is non-autocratic, ought to be desired.

Major premise (is—statement): The system of government that promotes widespread political participation is non-autocratic.

Conclusion (particular ought—judgement): The system of government that promotes widespread political participation ought to be desired.

This debate on the logical relationship between 'is' and 'ought' statements involves a range of issues, about whether 'ought' can be reduced to 'is', or derived from 'is', which falls outside the scope of the present study. Some social theorists, such as Habermas, have attempted to transcend this gulf by the argument that the validity claims in both the normative and propositional domains can be rationally examined through a process of argumentative discourse. This is possible, he argues because the validity claims in each of the domains presuppose reasons and grounds which can be advanced in their support, and can be given in response to criticism. Hence the validity claims in the propositional and normative domains are susceptible to rational argument. In his later work Habermas has moved from a neo-Hegelian towards a neo-Kantian position on this question of science and values, by recognizing more clearly the distinction between the two realms, though the tradition to which he belongs is very different from the neo-Kantian tradition of Rickert and Weber, where a subjective attitude is adopted towards the realm of values.

Other thinkers, such as Searle, have attempted to derive 'ought' from 'is', an attempt which has generated much debate amongst analytical philosophers, but this is a complex issue which goes beyond the scope of the present work. In this paper I have merely tried to clearify the confusion which treats normative as synonymous with utopian, and realistic as identical with value-neutral, and it is not necessary for the purposes of my argument that I should opt for either side in the debate on the naturalistic fallacy. For my purposes it is sufficient to demonstrate how the link between an is—statement and a particular ought-judgement (an all too familiar feature in social theory) is justified by the concealed universal ought-principle, and how through a process of logical regress it is possible to move from secondary to primary values and finally arrive at a conception of the 'good' society.

And it may be argued that even if I were to accept the logical rule that 'ought' cannot be derived from 'is', this acceptance would not necessarily imply the conclusion that science has no bearing on values. This is a misconception widely prevalent amongst realistic theorists, based, on the premise that science and values belong to two different worlds separated by a wide gulf and that cannot be bridged and that the acceptance of one implies the non-acceptance of the other; in short that one can either be concerned with 'fact' or with 'value.' From this point of view an argument is than advanced that democratic theory can either be empirical or normative, but not both, and the argument is then extended by the claim that since science provides an understanding of the real world of politics, therefore democraetic theorists who are interested in explaining the real world must choose the world of science, and reject that of values, which is utopian and unrealistic. This is an arroneous argument since it reduces into a simple dichotomy the range of issues involved in the relationship between science and values. What is lost right of is the fact that the rule of the separation between 'is' and 'ought' statements is only valid in the narrow region of the logical relationship between 'is' and 'ought', and the relationship between science and values involves a wider range of issues.

Science does have a bearing on value statements in many ways such as: (i) It can prove or disprove the factual premise in the syllogism, as shown above. (ii) It can examine the features of the descriptive component of a secondary value-statement. (iii) It can indicate the consequences that follow from either a primary or a secondary value position. And (iv) it can highlight 'inconvenient facts' which result from a value position. In the first syllogism, for example, science can empirically examine the claim that democracy is that system which ensures widespread political participation. It can investigate the institutional features of democracy, study the effects of widespread participation, and on the basis of this information determine whether these processes of politics satisfy the criteria of democracy initially considered to be valuable.

By examining these propositions of democracy science can generate information which may result in a conflict between two separate values in one value-sphere. For example, by showing that widespread participation may result in the violation of rights of minority by majority. Science indicates a possible conflict between (a) the value that widespread political participation ought to be desired and (b) the value that the rights of the minority ought not to be violated. If the second value stands higher in the hierarchy of values in a value-sphere, then science, by posing 'inconvenient facts', *i.e.*, showing that widespread participation may lead to the rights of the minority being violated, suggest that the value statement, 'widespread political participation ought to be desired', should be modified to 'widespread political participation ought to be desired but not if the rights of the minority are violated'.

Science can also indicate the means necessary to achieve a desired end. It can examine the social conditions required by the various means, show whether these conditions exist, suggest ways in which they can be maintained or brought about (as the case may be), and indicate which among competing means has the optimum chances of bringing about the end. Science can also highlight the consequences that follow from various ends. It can therefore: (i) identify appropriate means for the achievement of an end, (ii) indicate available alternatives such as the best balance between ends is achieved, and (iii) suggest the probable consequences that may follow from the adoption of any one value position. By providing more accurate information about the world it can also lead to more informed choices being made, to an increased sensitivity to the functioning of institutions, to a growth in concern for the outcome of policy, and to a greater awareness of the preferences of individuals, groups, and communities. By doing all this, science can detail the features and the consequences of the chosen 'good society'. What it cannot do, however, is to determine which of these conceptions of the good society is preferable to another.

It is the lack of clarity on this relationship between science and values which is responsible for the realistic theorists attempt to construct an empirical theory of democracy. Such an attempt seems to be based on the notion that since there is no logical relation between 'is' statements and 'ought' statements, science can have no effect on values, and thus value relativism becomes inevitable. To avoid such relativism, the realistic theorists attempted to construct a theory of democracy devoid of normative propositions, thus making their conception of democracy fully open to scientific analysis but this view, as I indicated above, has been shown to be untenable. Democratic theory has, inescapably, both a normative and an empirical component. Political science has a bearing on both components, more indirectly in the former case, as illustrated above, and more directly in the latter case inasmuch as it provides the tools for testing these empirical propositions.

A further attack on the attempt to construct a value-neutral democratic theory has come from philosophers of language, who argue that the words used to describe human situations are often words which have an evaluative component, an evaluative implication.[31] This is most evident in discussions of democracy where words like tyrannical, authoritarian, freedom, happiness, legitimacy, etc., are commonly used in the descriptive accounts of democratic processes. To say of an institution or of a form of behaviour, that it is tyrannical, is to condemn it, since tyranny in common usage, has come to represent a reprehensible form of authority. Such an argument is also valid in retation to other words. Though it is possible theoretically to replace such words by descriptions that do not have such an evaluative implication, *e.g.*, it may be possible to replace the word 'happiness' with 'that state of being indicated by laughter,' (though this does not seem to solve the problem and surely is no substitute) such a replacement does not only prove cumbersome, but also leads to a loss of accuracy and to a change in the meaning intended. Besides indicating the immensity of the task of replacing words whose usage implies commendation and approval, Taylor has argued further that there are some words like 'good' which are central to any discussion of the human situation, and which are unintelligible outside of any relationship to wants, needs and purposes. The attempt to purge langugae of words with an evaluative connotation thus would have such immense consequences for language, that it has not even begun to be considered. Hence for example, Lasswell and Kaplan's contention that 'the formulations throughout are descriptive rather than normatively ambiguous'[32] overlooks the existence of such words which have an evaluative connotation. In fact their discussion of democracy is replete with words such as 'exploitative', 'authoritarian', 'despotism', 'regimentation', etc., all of which certainly have an evaluative connotation. The word 'democracy' itself, indeed, in the modern world, has come to have such a character, since to say of a political process that it is 'democratic' implies approval, whereas to call it 'undemocratic', implies disapproval. Democracy has become a commendatory value word, as is evident from the fact that widely differing regimes across the world legitimize themselves by characterizing their functioning as being typical of 'real democracies.'[33]

The attempt to construct a value-neutral empirical theory of democracy has thus had very little success, but although the attempt may have been unsuccessful the impulse that motivated it still remains relevant. The techniques of investigation developed by science must be used to generate information and data which is more accurate, and corresponds better with the processes of democratic politics, than the impressionistic descriptions of politics which were present in 'classical' democratic theory. The call for a more realistic democratic theory is thus not an idle call, since testable propositions have no less an important function in democratic theory than do normative propositions.

Classical theories, on the one hand, did contain unrealistic notions such as 'collective will', 'common good', etc., which needed to be viewed afresh in the light of sociological evidence. Studies of voting behaviour and other aspects of political participation did provide insights into how individuals relate to, and comprehend, the processes of politics, and thus conceptions of human nature needed to be reassessed on the basis of such empirical information. Empirical theories, on the other hand, were far from value-neutral, since it was shown that they contained a value-slope that corresponded with the value-slope of the political systems that they had set out to investigate empirically. Such theories dismissed normative issues raised by political philosophy, and purported to be concerned only with the 'who gets what, when, and how' of democratic politics, but since they paid little attention to social change they tended to support the status quo. The conceptions of human nature implicit in these theories need to be examined more closely, and the criteria for deciding whether the features of these conceptions are realistic or utopian, valid or invalid, need to be more clearly specified, because a democratic theory which accepts the claim that science does have a bearing on values, in the ways indicated above, has then to confront the philosophical question: How does one decide which of the conceptions of human nature underlying the various theories of democracy is more realistic?[34]

Two conclusions follow from the discussions in this paper. The first is that political science can never replace political philosophy, since the nature of the questions asked by the latter are of a normative kind. Political science can, however, enrich, embellish, and extend political philosophy, providing a more realistic intellectual context within which the latter can pose its questions. The second conclusion is that science and values are inextricably linked in social explanation, although 'is' statements may differ in meaning and may be of a qualitatively different kind from 'ought' statements. This conclusion reinforces the claim made earlier that *all theories of democracy*, as distinct from particularistic explanations of democratic politics, have the following essential features: They all have (i) a notion of the 'good society'; either implicit or explicit, which expresses the ideal relationship between the individual and society. This notion of the 'good society' determines the value-slope of the theory; (ii) at least one value-statement which is either a preference or a value-judgement; and (iii) at least one descriptive statement of an explanatory kind indicating causality.

REFERENCES

1. Eulau, H., Eldersveld, S.J. and Janowitz, M. (eds) (1956). *Political Behaviour: a Reader in Theory and Research*, Glencoe, Ill: Free Press; Pool, I.S. (ed) 1967. *Contemporary Political Science: Towards Empirical Theary*, New York: Mcgraw-Hill; Ranney, A. (ed) 1962. *Essays in the Behavioural Study of Politics*, Urbna: University of Illinois Press.

2. Keat, R. (1981). *The Politics of Social Theory,* Oxford: Blackwell. p. 21.

3. P. Lasslett P. and Runciman W.G. (eds) *Philosophy, Politics, and Society* series 1-5, Oxford: Blackwell; Duncan, G. and Lukes, S. 1963. 'The New Democracy,' in *Political Studies,* vol XI, no 2, pp. 156-177; Macpherson, C.P. 1977. *The Life and Times of Liberal Democracy.*; Mostafa, Rejai. 1967. 'The Metamorphosis of Democratic Theory,' in *Ethics* vol 77, no 3, pp. 202-208; Pateman, C. 1970. *Participation and Democratic Theory.* Cambridge University Press; Taylor, C. 1972. 'Neutrality in Political Science' in Laslett, P and Runciman, W.G. (eds) *Philosophy, Politics, and Society,* 3rd series: Oxford: Oxford University Press; Skinner, Q. 1973. 'Empirical Theorists of Democracy and Their Critics,' in *Political Theory.* vol 1, no 3, pp. 287-306.

4. Bottomore, T.B. (1975). 'Conservative Man', in *Sociology as Social Criticism,* London: Allen and Unwin; Bachrach, P and M. Baratz. 1967. 'Two Faces of Power,' in McCoy, C. A. and J. Playford (eds) *A political Politics* New York: Thomas. Y. Crowell; Walker, J. 1971. 'A Critique of the Elitist Theory of Democracy,' in P. Bachrach (ed) *Political Elites in a Democracy,* New York: Atherton Press; Bowles, S. 1985. 'State Structures and Political Practices' in Coe, R.D. and Wilbur, C.D. (eds) *Capitalism and Democracy: Schumpeter revisited,* Indiana: University of Notre Dame Press.

5. Dahl, R.A. (1961). 'The Behavioural Approach in Political Science' in *American Political Science Review,* vol 55, p. 763.

6. *Ibid.* p. 764.

7. Among the early and more valuable studies of elections as a result of this new impetus, was the study of the 1940 presidential election by Paul. F. Lazarsfeld, Bernard Berelson and Hazel Gaudet, entitled *The People's Choice.* Published in 1944, and of the 1956 election by Angus Cambell, Philip Converse, Donald Stokes and Warren Miller, titled *The American Voter* (1960).

8. Dahl, R.A. (1961). 'The Behavioural Approach in Political Science.; Easton, D. 1969. The New Revolution in Political Science.' *American Political Science Review.* vol. 63, p. 1052.

9. Keat, R. (1981). *The Political of Social Theory.*

10. Pennock, J.R. and J.W. Chapman (eds). 1975. *Participation in Politics*, New York: Lierber-Atherton.

11. Pateman, C. (1970). *Participation and Democratic Theory*, p. 16.

12. Duncan, G and Lukes, S. (1963). 'The New Democracy,' p. 166.

13. Runciman, W.G. (1972). 'Sociological Evidence and Political Theory,' in *Philosophy, Politics and Society*. 2nd series.

14. Taylor, C. (1972). 'Neutrality in Political Science.' p. 40.

15. Wollheim, R. (1958). 'Democracy' in *Journal of the History of Ideas* vol 19, 1958, p. 233.

16. Berlin, I. (1972). 'Does Political Theory Still Exist?' in *Philosophy, Politics and Society*, 2nd Series. p. 8.

17. Duncan, G. and Lukes, S. (1963). 'The New Democracy.' p. 164.

18. White, D.M. (1979). ' "Negative" Liberty,' in *Ethics* vol. 80, p. 185-204; Macallum jr, G.C. 1972. "Negative" and "Positive" Freedom, in *Philosophy, Politics, and Society*, 4th Series.

19. Berlin, I. (1969). *Two Concepts of Liberty*. p. 126-7.

20. Taylor finds one major drawback in the conception of 'negative' liberty since it does not seem to consider the aspect of 'internal' intereference to do or be whatever the individual wishes to do or be. This draws attention to motivation, to the psychology of the subject, which may generate obstacles to action. Taylor attempts to show the implausibility of a minimum area of non-inter ference with action, and by doing so poses an interesting counter to Berl n's thesis of 'negative' liberty. Charles Taylor, 1969. 'What's Wrong with 'negative' Liberty', pp. 175-193. in Alan Ryan (ed) *The Idea of Freedom*. Oxford: Oxford University Press.

21. Berlin, I. (1969). *Two Concepts of Liberty*. p. 130.

22. Macpherson, C.B. (1969). 'The Maximization of Democracy" in *Philosophy, Politics, and Society* 3rd series. pp. 83-103. Macpherson distinguishes the different theories of liberal democracy as (i) those that justify a democratic system on the grounds that they maximize

individual utilities and (ii) those that justify a dsmocratic system on the grounds that they maximize individual powers. These differing justifications were premised on conceptions of human nature in the first case as an infinite appropriator and an infinite consumer because of infinite desires, and in the second case as a doer, a creator, an enjoyer ol his or her human attributes.

23. Quinton, A. 'Introduction' p. 20; Portridge, P.H. 1967. 'Politics, Philosophy, Ideology', p 32-52. in Quinton, A. (ed) *Political Philosophy*, Oxford: Oxford University Press.

24. Skinner, Q. (1973). 'Empirical Theorists of Democracy and their Critics.'

25. Walker, J. (1971). 'A Critique of the Elitist Theory of Democracy,' p. 70.

26. Taylor, C. (1969). 'Neutrality in Political Science', p. 40. Taylor bases his discussion on the argument that 'to say of something that it fulfils human needs, wants, or purposes always constitutes a *prima facie* reason for calling it "good." This raises a whole range of issues on human needs and politics and on what can be considered to be a real human need. These are issues that currently enjoy a revival in political theory, but which unfortunately I cannot go into here. R. Fitzgerald (ed). 1977. *Human Needs and Politics*, Sydney: Pergamon Press.

27. Hare, R.M. (1969). 'Descriptivism,' in W.D. Hudson (ed) *The 'is-ought' question*. London: Macmillan.

28. Weber, M. (1949). *The Methodology of the Social Science.*

29. Sen, A. (1970). *Collective Choice and Social Welfare.* chap. 5 'Values and Choice.' Holden-Day Inc. Interestingly there is in welfare economics a movement concurrent with and, similar to the 'New democracy' movement, which also seeks to rid welfare economics of values. Sen debunks the attempt by showing how it is not possible to purge welfare economics of value issues. Unfortunately he does not address the issue of the naturalistic fallacy.

30. A good introduction to the controversy on the 'is-ought' question from the interpretation of the original Human position, to the debate among philosophers of language, Searle, Hare, Foot, etc is

available in the collection by W.D. Hudson (ed) *The 'is-ought' Question* 1969. Macmillan.

31. *Ibid.* Part four: 'Description and Evaluation.'

32. Lasswell, H. and Kaplan, A. (1952). *Power and Society.* London: Routledge and Kegan Paul. p. 239.

33. Macpherson, C.B. (1966). *The Real World of Democracy.*

34. Forbes, I and Smith, S. (eds). 1983. *Politics and Human Nature.* London: Frances Pinter.

3

PLURALITY BALLOT AND BI-PARTY SYSTEMS, PROPORTIONAL REPRESENTATION AND MULTIPARTYISM: BETWEEN TRUE AND FALSE

GISELE DE MEUR

The Problem

The problem of the relationship between electoral systems and party systems came to the attention of the politicians and the political scientists as early as the second half of the nineteenth century. Long debates finally led scholars to some consensus on a less vague content, on less arbitrary arguments, on less partisan intentions which, since the end of World War II, Duverger summarised in the following condensed formulas: "The plurality single-ballot tends to party dualism" and "the run-off majority voting system and proportional representation tend to multipartyism."[1]

My attention to this problem was first drawn by discussions and correspondence with my colleague B. Owen; subsequently, my interest and enthusiasm grew, in particular after reading the works of D. Rae (1971), W.H. Riker (1976, 1982, 1986) and G. Sartori (1986). Their different points of view, and the talent with which they are exposed are as many searchlights pointed at a same hardly seizable reality. Their opposed enlightenments converge to a convincing image; the intention of this essay is to develop this picture as it appears to me as a result of these confrontations, and under the undoubtedly biased angle of my own vision. As I will only focus on a few steps of these author's reasonings, I must assume that the reader is familiar with their texts before he looks on to mine. Besides, if he is not, he is really missing something!

Riker (*1982*)[2]

To demonstrate the possibility of the accumulation of knowledge about politics, Riker retraces the history of the so-called Duverger problem. Both the main outlines of his proof and the methodological reflexions that go with it call for intellectual rally. Certainly we are faced with evidence of progressive scientific improvement, a process of reformulation and refinement of a social science problem, progressively separating its logical, empirical and ideological components. This should be argument against the myth of the lawless nature of human behaviour! Now, to reach a more dialectical and thus fruitful relation with Riker's analysis, we will have to go deeper into the problem and map out the limits of our agreement. Points of difference often suggest new analyses.

After stating both of Duverger's Laws, Riker's main effort tends to their clarification: three electoral systems are involved, and he describes the mechanisms of each; a relation between ballots and parties is enunciated, and Riker emphasizes the ambiguous and vague character of its formulation, the interpretation of which may vary between deterministic causality (and in which direction?), and probabilistic correlation. This had to be done. What is left unanalysed is a third part of the relationship, for which Sartori will vigorously criticize him. Sometimes it is referred to as the structure of the party system (p. 755), not otherwise specified, sometimes the discussion involves the number of political formations (p. 759) and at other places, it is dealt (the number of) parties represented in the national assembly. Not only are these variations of sense puzzling when he tries to apply a rigorous analysis; they just represent some out of the many possible ideas and above all they need precise and testable contours (I do not like the word "definition" but you see what I mean). I will revert to this later on.

After this, Riker explains how, simultaneously, the evolution of young Western democracies, their progression towards universal suffrage and the diversification of the electoral procedures initiated an awareness of the problem in question. He traces, in short, the succession of the opinions and arguments that evolved from an initial scepticism to a growing acceptance, towards an idea that followed "a gradual development culminating in a clear and unambiguous statement of both Duverger's propositions."

Let us not insist on "clear and unambiguous" now. What he suggests on this occasion (p. 755) is that different types of the electoral process motivate the candidates in an election differently, stimulating them, or not, to maximise their electoral support, and in so doing, creating, or not, favourable conditions for bi-party systems. Although not convinced by this explanation, I do not feel the necessity of discussing it here: it has no crucial bearing on subsequent developments. Moreover, it is not clear whether this minor weak point is just reported by Riker as an other received opinion, or if he really accepts it.

Certainly more puzzling are the several assertions criticised by Riker, where authors link Duverger's effects to such things as "(electoral systems) which confuse responsibility" the "practical capacity of the Anglo-Saxon Race" or "Indian activists being motivated more by the emotional satisfaction of membership and loyalty to the third party than by the rational search for political power." Now I suppose that these pieces of anthology cannot be taken seriously anymore and so let us come back to the very crexe of the issue. The principle of Riker's approach is the following: having stated as "semi-precise" the laws cited above, he confronts them with a number of counterexamples. From the choice of those, one can guess with some precision what Riker had in mind with regard to the less definite part of the laws; yet the game would have been made more simple, even if less captivating, it all basic concepts and hypotheses had been made more explicit.

First, he deals with the hypothesis that "PR and run-off majority voting favour multiparty systems." From the empirical and irreducible evidence of a number of counter-examples, he deduces that the hypothesis can at most be interpreted as a probabilistic association (as opposed to any causal deterministic relation or "universal law"). And he refers to Rae's (1971) analysis, offering a set of other major variables influencing the occurrence of multiparty systems under PR. Then Riker turns to rational choice theory (p. 759) and asserts that "PR and the second ballot run-off both offer politicians an incentive for the formation of new parties and do not give them any disincentive." As much I understand the meaning of the second, negative part of sentence—even if like Sartori, I would like it best with additional nuances, (see below), as much do I remain totally blind to the evidence of the first part; which objective incentive(s) are in play? It seems that the absence of disincentive has been taken into account twice by Riker, as if "not discouraging" was equivalent to "encouraging." And indeed, Riker himself must have been aware of this logical trap as he said that "neither feature of this incentive system is strong enough to permit one to say for certain that these electoral systems favour multiple parties. The incentive is weak because it operates only when people want to form new parties for other reasons."

So, let us put this argument to axe side.

Secondly, he comes to what he calls the more interesting question of the relationship between plurality elections and two-party systems. This time he qualifies the deviant cases as not definitive ones, and predicts that the law should "survive them with appropriate revisions." And he proposes such a revision in the form: "Plurality election rules bring about and maintain two-party competition except in countries where (1) third parties are continually one of two parties locally, and (2) one party among several is almost always the Condorcet winner in elections."

Leaving aside the form of this new law, on its substance I both agree and disagree: as I will suggest later, the way plurality elections act on national party competition is strongly dependent on local factors, such as the geographical division of constituencies, the existence of regional parties, and other parameters relating to the distribution of the electorate. On the other hand, I am not convinced about the story of the Condorcet winner. For this point, I am inclined to agree with Sartori that "Riker's second clause is not, as stated, an explanans but an explanandum," and that we still have to make another try to explain the exception(s). And is fact, this explanatory effort is taken somewhat further by Riker, showing once again that he is not the dupe of his own tricks. At this stage he refers to Duverger's distinction between two kinds of reasons for his laws to operate: a "mechanical effect" of under-representing losing parties and a "psychological effect" in that voters do not want to waste their votes on losers.

These two aspects of Duverger's law have now obtained full recognition among scholars, as long as one does not expect full agreement on what they individually impute to them. Further investigations show that there is a large spectrum of interpretations. Yet for this moment I will stick to Riker's own Building on indisputable arguments .he recalls empirical evidences of sophisticated voting in certain circumstances—and so we will take it as a fact, a fact whose occurrence depends on "initial conditions." The point where I depart slightly from his elaboration is the use he makes of "rationality," defined as the behaviour of an expected utility maximiser, successively applied to voters and to politicians. Not that I deny either the influence or the coherence of voters' and politicians' political choices, but rather that I would make the economy of maximisation, of utility and of expectation as technical explanatory tools. I can only consider them as metaphors for many different behaviours. Taken literally, they offer the danger of giving an *a priori* definition of what is rational, what is useful what is predictable (assuming which information?) . . . for every one of us. Of course, Riker does not do that. But a reading of Meehl (1977) convinced me that the danger should not be underestimated.

Why not simply say that the voter or the politician weighs the pros and cons before he settles his choice. Ordinary language produces no such sophisticated temptations as do technical terms; no one will try to throw weights on a scale to realize a choice simulation.

Now, this remark like the preceding ones, constitutes no criticism of the fundamentals of Riker's analysis—through which I persist to think that, truly, "there has been some accumulation of knowledge"!

Sartori (1986)

Taking the somewhat erratic course of Duverger's laws as a case study, Sartori questions whether "human behaviour is lawless to the extent of defying any and all attempts at construing "laws"—or is it that our methodological legs are atrophied"?

To answer this, Sartori's analysis covers three main areas:

—he sets out the subject, critically recalls previous formulations, discussions and evolutions, reviewing thirty years of literature. In particular, he comments on Rae's and Riker's contributions.

—he frames the methods, and outlines both how past failures can be attributed to faulty tools of analysis and what improvements could result from greater care.

—he then brings these two aspects together and reconstructs the arguments leading to a new understanding of the laws relating the link between electoral system and party systems.

Throughout his analysis is carried out with an uncompromising rigour, clarity and logic; but I will suggest occasionally Sartori's vigorous criticism needs further comment.

Let us start with his remarks about Rae and Riker. My impression is that Sartori does not do justice to Rae, on several points.

With a constant empirical concern, Rae's book tends to show up which part of the observed facts can be explained as consequence of the formal electoral rules acting on formal party systems. That is to say that parameters like the ideological spectrum of parties, the degree of establishment of parties among the electorate, the type of diffusion of information, and so many others. . . are not taken into account, while format characteristics, such as the number of parties, their respective electoral support (in numbers of voters), the sizes of the constituencies, etc . . . are referred to invariably.

Still more obvious is that Rae attempts to describe what really occurs in his data, and to put forward observed consequences, following an inductive procedure; Rae does not assess any affirmation predicting what can logically occur, which would come out of a deductive proceeding. However, the study of "what is" does not conflict with considerations about frequencies (I did not say "probabilities"), with correlation computations, with tendency laws admitting exceptions. These elaborations have, by nature no definitive status, they tolerate the instability of facts, they are an essential first step to constructing explanations. In contrast, the study of "what could be" is of logical nature, and within a predetermined framework, proceeds deductively; its laws bear no exceptions, but they can allow themselves to start by an "if."

So, when Sartori says (p. 45) "(. . .) if the problem is (. . .) the accumulation of knowledge, (. . .) then Rae can hardly be said to belong to such a cumulative process", I wonder why. The answer follows: "the methodological approach of Rae is entirely different from the one of Duverger—and it is here that the "accumulation" entirely breaks down. Duverger has causal "laws" in mind; Rae never uses the word cause (except to reject it) and very deliberately speaks of "propositions" that assert, in turn, a wide gamut of linkages ("tends to", but also "associates with", "almost always", but also "often")."

If Sartori summarises the authors' writings well and currently points to their differences, on the other hand, his conclusions are rather strange. Causal analysis deals, for a large part, with logic and Rae deals with empirical data, in which—along with the merit of having assembled them—he has the talent to provide it a semblance of order. The patient and meticulous astronomic observations of Tycho Brahe nourished the savant speculation of Kepler Rae's book offers ready-to-use data to test against theoretical constructions and there is no need to deny its participating in the "accumulation of knowledge" process.

In a sense, I could go along with Sartori in saying: "All in all, it cannot be said that Rae builds upon Duverger: he attends to an entirely different thing": different but not alien. Rae does not build upon anyone, he constructs new foundations.

Pursuing the comparison, Sartori adds: "A major difference bears also on how the effects of the causal factors are conceived (. . .) Now if Duverger is to be criticized because laws must declare effects that are specific enough to allow testing, the same criticism applies even more to Rae's propositions."

This looks like a double contradiction. First, Rae does not make use of "causes"—as Sartori pointed out!—because he does not attempt to prove laws. Secondly, one may not be simultaneously responsible for lack and excess in specifying properties. Let me illustrate this. Under the plurality rules Rae observes a collection of party systems. If, for clarifications sake categories of party systems are then drawn, cutoff points must be chosen. Rae chooses to define two-party systems as those in which the first party holds less than 70 per cent of the seats, and the first two parties together, at least 90 per cent (of the seats). The property is considered at one point in time not as a long-standing-trend feature. This is specific enough to decide whether a party system is, or is not, a two-party system in the sense of Rae. And that is all one can of a definition. Besides this, Rae's analysis belonged to in the domain of observed facts, not of logical demonstration. So one can start a second reading, another ordering, different analogies of the empirical material—and if new data is added, or if new categories are chosen (with 89 per cent instead of 90 per cent, why not?), they do not break down the old scaffolding—contrary to counter-examples in a logical reasoning, which annihilate the proof—but they supplement to it. Of course, there is no doubt that science's progress also needs a more speculative counterpart to empirically established regularities; no doubt either that adjusting the two images of this two-folded mirror is most important, otherwise reality remains unexplained and explanations remain unreal.

Now, let us turn to a second area. Concerning Riker, Sartori starts off with disagreement on several points of principle, mainly concerning probalistic versus deterministic statements, laws and causal relations, necessary and sufficient conditions.

Let us say that, at different moments, both Riker and Sartori are walking in a very disputed area! It all begins with a comment by Riker (p. 761) on his own revised law (cited above). "Note that this formulation is deterministic—an attempt to avoid the ambiguity of Duverger and Rae. The law asserts that, with the exceptions noted, the plurality rule is a sufficient condition for a two-party system. It is not, however, an assertion of a causal relation, in as much as plurality rule is not a necessary condition (vide, Austria)."

Sartori comments: "What is a "deterministic" law that does not assert a "causal relation"? In turn, why is it that failing a "necessary condition," and yet having a "sufficient condition," we do not have a "causal relation"?"

I will not inquire deeply into the question of the "deterministic" law. I guess that Riker's intention was to stress that the exceptions which mattered in the previous formulations were eliminated in his own version. I will also comment very briefly on definitions, avoiding metaphysical puzzles. Sartori begins his essay and develops his third paragraph with—normative?—statements about scientific laws, where, in short, he links their explanatory power to their causal-type content. Under what condition(s) a scientific finding will be called a "law" is a pure matter of definition. And Sartori has a right to give a definition for scientific laws. Consistency will then force him to respect his own rules whenever he will evoke such laws. But the obligation does not apply to authors who did not sign the convention!

The next step is more complex. Let me try first to outline Riker's argument. The existence of examples where two-party competition is observed without plurality election rules shows that plurality rule is not a necessary condition for bipartyism. Thus, even if it were to be considered as a cause of bipartyism, it could certainly not be considered as the cause of it. Other causes must exist, unless we admit that something can sometimes occur without cause. Now, also Sartori's reaction can be understood. He asks: "Why does a necessary condition (*i.e.*, a condition stated negatively) establish a causal link, whereas a sufficient condition (a condition that suffices to produce an effect) does not?"

First, from a logical point of view, both a necessary condition and a sufficient condition translate as an implication.

A is a necessary condition for B means that $A \Leftarrow B$, while

A is a sufficient condition for B means that $A \Rightarrow B$.

Only the direction of the implication is reversed. Then why should we, indeed, impute to the one attributes we would refuse to the other?

Second, one common understanding of causality, or more precisely of "A causes B", is that whenever A occurs, so does B, that is to say "$A \Rightarrow B$" *i.e.* A is a sufficient condition for B.

There we are. After that attempt to advocate for the devil, it may look as if the gordian knot was even more tightly fastened.

Now, remember: all men are mortal, Socrates is a man, thus Socrates is mortal. We can write as well: man$\Rightarrow$mortal, etc. . .

Are we seeing here a cause of mortality? Or any kind of explanation of it? Here we have a reason for making a clear distinction: a logical implication is not equivalent to a causal relation. Implication is a well defined concept, apt to be established by logical proof, or denied with the same unambiguity. The discovery of "causes" is not so simple. Nevertheless, this is not to say that scientific discourse has to banish definitely any reference to causal relations. But the normal terms used to describe causality are highly polysemic and provoke imprecision and misunderstanding; I thus fear that many of us will have to sacrifice to the altar of scientific precision much of their taste for concision and elegence. It is a pity but double meanings and omissions weaken science as much as they do invigorate poetry!

One more word about logic. Given that he later devotes a substantial paragraph to introduce precise logical concepts, I wonder why Sartori writes (p. 50): "All the necessary and sufficient conditions for an event to occur may be present, and yet nothing happens." What is the signification of "all the necessary and sufficient conditions"? Are we in presence of condition(s) that are both necessary and sufficient?And what is meant by "all" conditions? Moreover, if one single sufficient condition occurs, the event must follow. As we now deal with logical, well defined, terms, rigid and univocal significations apply. . . But this is enough.

If on the one hand, I have expressed some reservations about Sartori's methodological remarks, on the other, I was greatly reassured by the manner in which he puts them to use. His criticisms may be severe but his own analysis is carefully weighted and nuanced. In this third area, I will emphasize on three special points, respectively concerning plurality rules, PR towards plurality and proportional representations.

Most important is certainly the following (pp. 54, 55): (. . .) the plurality formula conditions the voter (. . .). This means that the voter's choice (unless he prefers to waste his vote) is concretely restricted, very often, to the front-runners. Hence, the plurality single-member district system does indeed "manufacture" and contrive, constituency by constituency, two-party competition. But if the voter is restrained (vis-a-vis his first and unfettered preferences), a reductive effect on the total number of national parties by no means necessarily follow. (. . .) The question thus becomes: under what conditions does a political system pass from local bipartyism to national bipartyism?" This question and its premises will in fact be the subject of our last paragraph.

Sartori's answer to clear: "Since the effect of the electoral system is a constituency effect, it is clearly the case that a necessary condition is missing and that we must search for at least another factor or variable. And the missing variable is the party system itself." Instead I shall argue that plurality systems have entirely different mechanical effects (beyond the district) depending on the geo-political repartition of the electorate. And that is to me the only direct missing factor.

The question of the complex relationship between geographical distribution of partnership and party systems, mutually interacting, is certainly worth a thorough study, but I will not go into it now. Sartori's text gives a few hints in this direction, and these could help further analysis.

Next point. Let us notice the following congruence of opinions. Sartori (p. 53) points that: "the size of the constituency (measured by the number of candidates is elects) affects the proportionality of PR more than do the various mathematical translation formulas" and: "the smaller the district the lesser the proportionality and, conversely, the larger the district the greater the proportionality."

And now, Differential Proposition Ten by Rae (1971, p. 115). "The proportionality with which legislative seats are allocated increases in relation to the magnitude of electoral districts: the higher the magnitude, the greater the proportionality." What should surprise us here is not the similarity between these two propositions in their true parts, but the persistence of their agreement on what is less true. This is not to say that I disagree with the latter general idea, far from it. When considered as describing a general tendency, true "on average", both forms of the statement seem obvious. But when dealing with particular cases, more caution reveals itself necessary.

Consider the following simplified situation: Three parties A, B and C compete for the election of 32 representatives, and the electorate's geo-political distribution is uniform across the country (this assumption is necessary to isolate the only parameter now being tested, *i.e.*, the magnitude of constituencies).

The proportional rule to translate votes into seats is D'Hondt's allocation method.[3]

— Imagine first that the unique electoral district is the whole country, thus having to elect the 32 representatives as a whole.
Four election simulations have been plotted (see figure 1) to illustrate, among other things, numerical differences concerning the parties' respective strength. For clarity, the alphabetical order will also denote the order of vote shares. The first row of the figure gives, for each of the four examples, the percentages of votes earned by the parties, the second row indicates their (strictly proportional) deserved quotas of seats, and the third row illustrates the actual allocation of seats.

— Now suppose that the country is divided into two electoral districts (constituencies) of indentical size—each having thus to elect 16 representatives. The resulting allocation of seats is given in row four of figure 1.

— Then let us continue by the same division process, to consider successively the cases of 4, 8, 16 and 32 (equally sized) constituencies (rows 5 to 8 of figure 1).

Reading the figure vertically gives an idea of the evolution of the representation under electoral rules degenerating from pure PR (ideal quotas) to a single member plurality system. Example 1 shows a monotonic tendency, as the number of constituencies rises, for the big party A, to gain at the cost of the small parties B and C. The other examples, in contrast, show how the general trend may be more random. Example 2 involves three parties of medium strength (about one third of the total votes for each); yet the course of party B is quite irregular, fluctuating between over-and under-representation. Example 3, with one large and two small parties, gives a case where the smallest party C will benefit from a small-scale constituency (getting 8 seats for constituencies of size 4 instead of 6 seats for the whole country constituency). Finally, example

4 with a small party C opposed two large front-runners, shows the third party rapidly losing any representation.

As a conclusion, to say that proportionality increases with the magnitude of districts is generally true (on average), as a tendency, but the function is not necessarily monotonic *i.e.* it may sometimes decrease inside the general increasing trend. And it has also been noticed that a large party, as well as a small party, may suffer from under representation on the road from plurality to pure proportional representation.

To conclude these remarks, I cannot but agree with Sartori's definitive clarification about PR's influences, when he says (p. 58): "pure PR is a no-effect electoral system. Conversely PR affects the party system to the extent that it is non-proportional and this on a variety of counts: the relatively small size of the constituencies, clauses of exclusion, majority premiums, and, lastly, disproportional translations of the votes into seats. It follows from this that whenever PR obtained manipulative effects, these effects are restrictive, not multiplicative. Hence, the influence of PR merely represents an enfeeblement of the same influence that is exerted by the majority—plurality systems." All this is fully consistent with the observation of the general trend from pure PR to plurality rule when the size of the constituencies decreases. And if we adopt Sartori's terminology, terming as "strong electoral system" those highly susceptible to exerting a manipulative influence and "feeble electoral systems" those exerting no such influence, clearly plurality rules qualify as strong systems and pure PR as feeble systems. More precisely, this should be put as "plurality systems possess an important potentiality for distorting in the translation of votes into seats, while pure PR does not." And, of course this distortion, which can occur in both directions (under—and over—representation) and on any party—depending on the geopolitical distribution—can only, with regard to the number of parties, reduce if not conserve it.

For more arguments on the numerous points where I find myself in agreement with Sartori, have an attentive look at his brilliant demonstration; for the remaining points, *go through the last paragraph.*

Figure 1

		EX. 1	EX. 2	EX. 3	EX. 4
% votes	A	58.21	35.21	50.05	48.00
	B	27.50	33.75	29.97	42.00
	C	14.29	31.04	19.98	10.00
quotas	A	18.63	11.27	16.02	15.36
	B	8.80	10.80	9.59	13.44
	C	4.57	9.93	6.39	3.20
1 district x 32 — seats A B C		19 9 4	11 11 10	16 10 6	16 13 3
2 districts x 16 — seats A B C		20 8 4	12 10 10	16 10 6	16 14 2
4 districts x 8 — seats A B C		20 8 4	12 12 8	20 8 4	16 16 0
8 districts x 4 — seats A B C		24 8 0	16 8 8	16 8 8	16 16 0
16 districts x 2 — seats A B C		32 0 0	16 16 0	16 16 0	16 16 0
32 districts x 1 — seats A B C		32 0 0	32 0 0	32 0 0	32 0 0

A touch of Mathematics

This paragraph is devoted to the influence of the plurality rule on the representation of parties. First of all, several preliminary points should be settled. The two following points should not be confused, the "mechanical" effect of the electoral rule, and its "psychological" effect. The mechanical effect works on the transformation of votes into seats and shows up as the possible bias (measured against strict proportional representation) it brings about through this operation. The psychological effect concerns the reactions of both voters and politicians to a particular system; the voter may try to vote strategically (*e.g.*, to vote for a second choice when he forecasts that his preferred candidate has no chance of winning and the politician may hesitate or decline to stand for a seat he has no chance of winning.

The existence of sophisticated voting has been shown empirically in many surveys. These references have also shown that the proportion of voters using such sophisticated voting does not depend only on the electoral system. Other factors include the estimated chances of the preferred candidate, the ideological distance between first and second choice, the differences in strength between two major parties within the constituency, etc, . . . So I will take it as a fact, that it occurs under specific conditions, and that it needs no attempt of any kind of justification, like being a behaviour imposed by some rational or moral imperative.

There is no gainsaying the fact that the two effects interact: the mathematical bias brought by the rule acts on peoples' strategies and these reactions in turn, by modifying the voting situation, alter the mechanical effect of the rule (by, for instance, reinforcing it). Yet the nature of the interaction will not be fully grasped until each of its two components has been paid some (individual) attention.

With this in mind, I will now investigate independently the second factor of influence, *i.e.*, the mechanical effect. To demonstrate this, I *will make* use of a simple mathematical model. The model must be considered as an over-simplified figure, sketching the workings of a mechanism—not as an attempt to reproduce any real event. It is aimed at giving an understanding of how things happen, even though they may not happen in such a simple way.

The questions are:

—to what extent can a plurality system influence an election outcome (by simple distortion in the translation of votes into seats)?

—can these distortions take the appearance (and thus explain): bi partyism crushing third (weak) parties, one, partyism obtaining an undue majority (of seats) or multi-partyism possibly distorted (in comparison with the proportions of votes)?

The need for answering these questions follows from the following fact: if we know three competing parties respectively receive:

A: 40 per cent, B: 45 per cent and C: 15 per cent of the total votes we still have no idea about the distribution of seats among the parties (4). Contrary to pure PR, nothing can be said without specifying the distribution of partisans for each party in each constituency.

So let us see how it works, under simplifying hypotheses, for an imaginary party P.

The following assumptions and definition are used:

(HI)—each constituency has the same population size (measured as the number of voters);

(H2)—party P receives a percentage p of the total (national) vote;

(H3)—the electorate is homogeneously—bipartitioned" with respect to party P, *i.e.*, in a percentage of c constituencies, P receives a constant (geographically uniform) percentage π of the votes;

while elsewhere (percentage of $1-c$ constituencies), P receives no vote; (thus $\pi=p/c$ and its bounds are $p\leqslant\pi\leqslant1$.)

(H4)—an index for the regional concentration is given by

$$r=\frac{1-c}{1-p};$$

obviously the extreme values for r are:

$r=0$ if P has a nationwide uniform partisanship:

$c=1,\ \pi=p$;

$r=1$ if P has a unanimous support in its electoral bastions:

$c=p,\ \pi=1$;

(H5)—three are three parties competing for the election. (similar models may be formulated for any number of parties, but their number has to be known).

Suppose that party P has obtained 15 per cent of the votes, with no assumption on the other parties' shares of the votes, then the following points hold:

—if P's partisans are all grouped on 15 per cent of constituencies, where they are unanimous, then P receives 15 per cent of the seats.

—if P's partisans are uniformly dispersed across the country, with 15 per cent of the voters in each constituency, then by (H5), P receives no seat at all.

—and for intermediate situation of P, what is the best it may hope?

. The thriftiest way to win a seat in a three-party competition is to get one third of the votes plus one, while the two other competitors share equally the rest of the votes. This optimal situation for P can at most happen in a percentage of 3p constituencies (when the number of voters is sufficiently large), that is P's maximum maximorum is to win 45 per cent of the seats. This (unachieved) limit case corresponds to $p=0.15$, $c=0.45$, $\pi=0.333 \ldots$, $r=0.647 \ldots$

. All situations in which P's concentration is weaker than above will imply no seat for P.

This corresponds to $p=0.15$, $0.45 \leqslant c \leqslant 1$, $0.15 \leqslant \pi \leqslant 0.33$, $0 \leqslant r \leqslant 0.647 \ldots$

. When π attains 50 per cent or more, party P, is ensured as many seats as constituencies where it has partisans, *i.e.*, a percentage of seats equal to c.

This corresponds to $p=0.15$, $0.3 \leqslant c \leqslant 0.5$, $0.5 \leqslant \pi \leqslant 1$, $0.823. \leqslant r \leqslant 1$

. Finally, when π lies between 0.15 and 0.5, the most that can be won by P is a percentage c of the seats, which can only occur if no other party can reach as much as P in the constituencies that give it some favour. Of course, nothing guarantees achieving this upper bound; on the contrary, under less favourable circumstances, P may also get no seat.

The above points are synthesized—and hopefully clarified—in Figure 2. Figure 2 shows the relationship between π and c, given that $p=0.15$: the curve is a rectangular hyperbola given by the equation $\pi. c=0.15$, and bounded, as already shown, by $0.15 \leqslant c \leqslant 1$ and $0.15 \leqslant \pi \leqslant 1$. Figure 2b shows the evolution of the maximum proportion of seats (M) that can possibly be won by party P, in relation to the parameter π (5). It is most important to keep in mind that two kinds of information are shown on the graph: the dotted part of the curve stands for a contingent relation, thus endowed with probabilities whose values decrease when M increases, while the two heavy lines indicate certain events.

Figure 2a

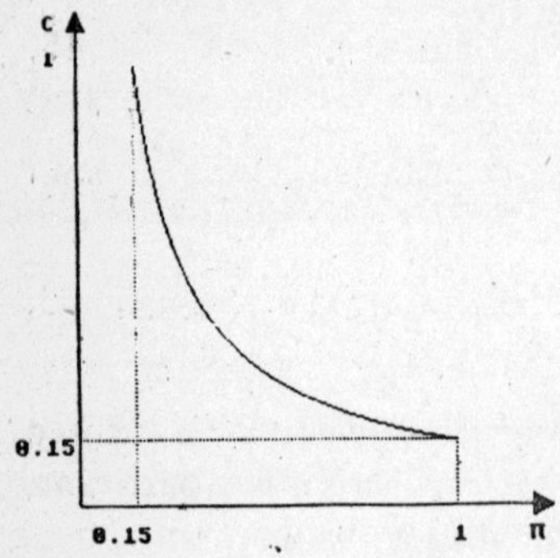

Figure 2b

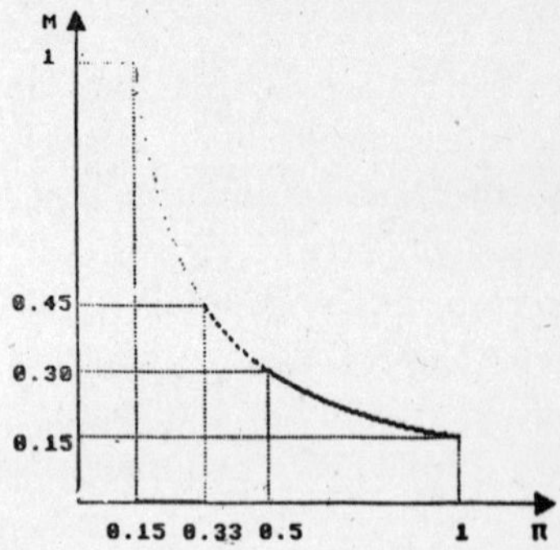

We can now summarize the points made above. Bearing in mind the picture given by the previous model, it is easy to figure out how such cases as "distorted multipartyism (a), overwhelming bipartyism (b) or usurping monopartyism (c) "can occur, as I shall instance by particular examples. Let me insist that the occurrence of situations of types (a), (b) or (c) does not depend upon the restrictions imposed by the hypothesis of our model: the reductive form of our axioms was merely aimed at simplifying without affecting the fundamentals of the distortion process. To make it very clear, I will exhibit examples taken in an "ordinary" election context, free from any specific model constraints. Furthermore, the choice of constituencies of variable sizes (in number of voters) would only have been a factor of reinforcement of the imbalance between seats and votes shares; I decided to avoid this aggravating circumstance by choosing equally sized constituencies. The more isolated the cause of the bias, the more convincing its very nature, which I want to prove as being the electoral rule.

Examples: imagine that parties A, B and C compete for the seats of 6 constituencies C_i; in each of the three following situations the *global* percentage of votes earned by the parties will be. 50 for A, .35 for B and .15 for C; *indicates the winner in each constituency.

We can see in this light that bipartyism is not necessarily the rule, with the other alternatives being exceptions; rather, all the alternatives constitute a part of a more general rule. Now. to go from here to an exhaustive analysis of all the situations that will result in each of these outcomes requires a further step. The degree of concentration (6) of each competing party certainly contains some helpful information; but the real situation is irreducibly two-dimensional and no single unidimensional index will thus suffice to embrace it. This problem is still open.

. case (a): distorted multipartyism

		A	*B*	*C*
local distribution	cl	.90*	.10	0
of *votes*	c2	.80*	.20	0
(in percentages *or*	c3	.35	.55*	.10
in absolute numbers,	c4	.35	.60*	. 5
with suitable units)	c5	·34	.30	·36*
	c6	.26	.35	.39*
Global distribution of *seats*		2	2	2
comparison votes		.5	.35	.15
(%) seats		.333. . .	.333 . . .	.333 . . .
		(under-representation)	(fair)	(over-represnta-tion)

. Case (b): overwhelming bipartyism

A	B	C
.60*	.40	·25
.55*	.25	. 5
.50*	.35	.10
.50*	.15	.20
.40	.45*	.15
.35	.50*	.15
4	*2*	0
.5 .666 . . .	.35 .332 . . .	.15 0

. Case (c): usurping monopartyism

A	B	C
.98*	.02	0
.34	.30	·36*
.34	.35*	.31
.44	.50	. 6
.45	.46*	. 9
·45	·47*	. 8
1	*4*	*1*
.5 .1666. . .	.35 .666. . .	.15 .1666. . .

NOTES

1. Numerous versions of Duverger's Laws have appeared 9 and will not retrace their history; the form I set here is just aimed at giving the general idea they all carried. Likewise, I will not go into the subtle question of whether Duverger did or did not grant his two propositions different scientific statuses (he affirms he did not). Nor will I search for exact dating or true paternity. None of these elements will intervene further and no argument will hinge upon the formulation in itself. Only the meaning—or the lack of it—will be concerned.[7]

2. A revised version of the text has now appeared in Grofman and Lijphart (Eds), 1986, but no major changes appear to me; thus, I still refer to the initial paper published in APSR, to facilitate later comparisons with Sartori's comments on it.

3. D'Hondt's allocation method (or highest average formula) may be described as follows, as a recurrent procedure: the seats in a district are awarded one at a time, to the party presenting the "highest average," *i.e.*, the greater quotient q, where

$$q = \frac{\text{(number of votes earned by the party)}}{\text{(number of seats already allotted to the party)} + 1}$$

4. Until now, I did not want to specify the sense of the word "party" —but it is now time to say that I mean it in a purely electoral context: a party is a group competing as such in the electoral process, and recognized as such by the electorate, whether it may be institutional or not, as in the ease of proportional—list ballot, by some seat allocation rule, some label, etc . . .

5. The Figure 2c could synthesize Figure 2a and Figure 2b.

6. Rae proposed (p. 154, 156) the following definitions: "a party's absolute concentration is the proportion of its total national vote concentrated in its "best" district. And second, its relative concentration is this proportion divided by the proportion of the electorate at large found within the same district." This kind of indices have the advantage of being well-defined in realistic cases—while my index r needs the hypotheses of the model to be computed. Yet Rae's

indices have the obvious weakness of depending only on the mode of the distribution of the party's electorate.

Figure 2c

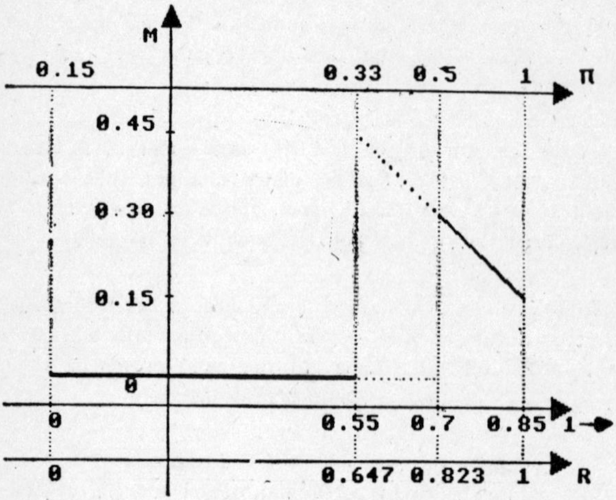

REFERENCES

Grofman, B. A. Lijphart and (editors) (1986), Electoral Laws and their Political Consequences, Agathon Press, New York.

Meehl, P.E. (1977), The Selfish Voter Paradox and the Thrown—Away Vote Argument, The American Political Science Review 71, pp. 11—30.

Rae, D.W. (1967), revised 1971), The Political Consequences of Electoral Laws, Yale University Press, New Haven and London.

Riker, W.H. (1976), The Number of Political Parties, A Re-examination of Duverger's Law, Comparative Politics 9, pp 93—106.

—(1982, revised 1986 in Grofman—Lijphart, eds.), The Two—party System and Duverger's Law: an Essay on the History of Political Science, The American Political Science Review 76, pp. 753—766.

Sartori, G. (1986), The Influence of Electoral Systems: Faulty Laws or Faulty Method?, in Grofman and Lijphart (eds.) pp. 43—68.

Part II

Democracy in the Third World

4

THE BACKGROUND OF DEMOCRACY: STATE-BUILDING IN BRAZIL AND ARGENTINA

HELGIO TRINDADE

The controversy over the relationship between state and society was the one which most polarized the Brazilian social scientists in the last years. The traditional cleavage emerged from the comparison between the position of Raymundo Faoro who emphasizes the role of the State by the "bureaucratic layer of society" throughout the "formation of Brazilian patronage" and those of Sergio Buarque de Holanda e Nestor Duarte for whom the pivotal issue was the agrarian society and its ways of private ownership. (Holanda, 1969; Duarte 1939). The monistic presuposition in this double hermeneutic source (which marks to a great extent, the subsequent development of the debate) caused the inconvenience—in spite of the richness of the suggested hypothesis—of severely restrain "the possibility of reconstructing the historical processes in terms different from the dual terms of the debate.

The most recent version of the debate has broken, to a large extent, with the parameters of the previous dichotomization when critically discussing the validity of certain historical inferences (Iglesias, 1976; Carvalho, 1979) and did the same with the concepts of (capitalism and feudalism when analysing the formation of Brazilian agrarian society. The important thing, however, was that the controversy itself gave rise to new approaches to the study of the State—society issue, thus generating richer interpretations of Brazilian society in terms of political process. In this sense the contribution of S. Schwartzman was really stimulating; in this book Base do Autoritarismo Brasileiro, Schwartzman retakes Faoro's thesis about state hegemony within a neopatrimonialistic perspective, attempting (through the concept of political cooptation) to explain how the state manages to make autonomous forms of participation submitted to its tutelage.

Certainly the thesis of the deep rootage of "authoritarianism" in South America is strongly based on reality, although the indiscriminate use of such concept to characterize different political situations make it as fluid as "populism." The sometimes excessive preoccupation to emphasize the authoritarian aspects in the political systems also impaired our capacity to understand the processes and strategies of liberal kind (except Santos, 1978) which are present in Latin-American politics. Liberalism has also been a manifest and perceivable trait in the political and ideological institutions ever since the colonial days (and as far as Brazil is concerned liberalism permeates both the republican and the monarchic periods) thus making it necessary to analyse the articulation of the process of state formation and the liberal dynamics. This paper, however, aims at a preliminary phase; the paper tries to discuss, besides the structural variables mentioned in the literature the factors which measured the process of state formation during the nineteenth century, the Brazilian and Argentinean situation being compared.

The Construction of the State

All analyses of the formation of the national State insist on its origin in the feudal society in transition towards capitalism and, at the same time, on the European specificity of the State phenomenon (Anderson, 19878; Badie, Birnbaum, 1979; Strayer, 1979).

Overlooking the discussion on historical frontiers of the statization (state-making) process, it seems legitimate to postulate the effective existence of national states in Latin America even though their structure, unlike the European tradition, is closely connected to the colonial fact and its political heritage. Although most experts question the presence of "feudalism" in the area, this does not exclude the formation of national state nor does it render the utilization of that concept in the Latin-American context invalid, even though some qualifications concerning differences, for example, in State formation in areas of Spanish settlement and Portuguese settlement are necessary.

State formation in peripheral societies (particularly Latin America) also escapes the classical conception of State as a reflex of civil society. His analysis shows that "the more belated the insertion of the State in the world market and the attempts to define and achieve its economic development, the more decisive and extended the role of the State system in countries of the third world." Consequently, in Latin America, besides the fact that the State plays a more important role in the capitalistic centre, the national dominant class is the daughter of the state apparatus. Moreover, the state is not the idealized synthesis of the existing civil society; on the contrary, its primary function is to be "the agent of a synthesis" in a society deeply heterogeneous (O'Donnel, 1980).

Although O'Donnel's analysis points out some central elements in the determination of the Latin American State specificities (weight of the colonial heritage, insertion in the world market, effect on the structuralization of social domination etc.) it does not refer to other factors which were also relevant in Latin America. I would like to mention especially the internal dynamics of the economy; the relation between regional areas, "centre" and national unity; the profile of the political elites and their degree of autonomy in relation to the economically dominant classes; the dissociation between the civil and religious powers, the influential power of the Army or military of the bureaucracy forces, etc.

The comparison between Brazilian and Argentinean political systems shows that there are different patterns of "political development" in these two countries. On the one hand, the Argentinean pattern indicates a belated process of National State formation, whereas in Brazil the state was precociously constituted. On the other hand, as far as liberal dynamics is concerned the above pattern is inverted; while in Argentina the rhythm of expansion of the political arena is stronger and broader, in Brazil it develops in a slow and restricted way.

Ever since the colonial days two structural aspects which are important to the understanding of the Brazilian and Argentinean cases have become apparent. First the organization of an independent economy has produced a significant effect on its spatial distribution. In Argentina such articulation was relatively restricted if compared to the broader internal connection in the Brazilian economy (Furtado, 1976). Second, the weight of the institutional political-administrative legacy was different in the Brazilian case, the more complex colonial administrative apparatus generated a bureaucratic system (Faoro, 1958) and was transmitted in its totality because of the peaceful transition towards Independence. Argentina because of its condition as a belated viceroyalty (1776) inherited a simpler and decentralized institutional structure because of the type of metropolitan control. Also the structure at first adopted (with the deposition of the Vice-king in Buenos Aires) was totally modified by the prolonged and conflictive process of national unification. The importance of such colonial traits becomes then fully evident.

In Argentina, the absence of a better and broader articulation between the economy and the territory occupation, as well as the loose and decentralized relation with Spain, has probably affected the belated formation of the State despite the precocity of the national independence. Conversely, the diversification of the Brazilian economy during the period of mining decadence as well as the long tradition of centralized control of the colonial institution has favoured the complexity and the rapidity of the State configuration. The rupture of the colonial link has made it crucial for both countries to create a centre which may bring about conditions for the appearance of a state structure.

If some factors as we have seen are linked to the colonial period (differences in the economical political—administrative structures) others result from the way the political emancipation happened. First, both countries become independent in different ways: Brazil conquers political implication rapidly, between 1822 and 1825 (after the northeastern republican movement known as Confederation of the Equador in Pernambuco was defeated) while in Argentina ten years elapsed between the "portena insurrection" and the final war of independence. Second, internal politics evolve in a completely different way on one hand, "the typically Brazilian scheme of continuity in relation to the colonial administration"; on the other hand, "the rather violent discontinuity inherent to the Spanish-American America" (O'Donnel, 1980) such variations are not only explained by the colonial past, but also by the period after the independence, resulting in two distinct effects: the permanence of the political unity in Portuguese America and the territorial fragmentation of Spanish America.

To a large extent, the political systems established in former Spanish colonies, faced a "long anarchic period and many of them would only organize the ruling power on relatively legitimate bases by means of caudillo—type leadership." In the Brazilian case, "if an initial period of instability and rebellions could not have been avoided, at least a violent and irregular change of governments never took place (if the abdication and the anticipations of the Emperor's legal age are not considered violent and irregular) and the supremacy of the civil power has always been maintained (Carvalho, 1980:15).

As a consequence, the support of the monarchy by the Brazilian political elite made the transition easier and created a basic consensus among the governing class, thus garanting a reasonable level of legitimacy and stability for the new regime, legitimacy and stability being indispensable for the preservation of the national unity.

In Argentina, on the contrary, if there was unanimity for the declaration of independence there was no unanimity as to the type of government which the United Provinces should adopt (Romero, 1979:68). The absence of a clear definition of the emerging state territorial frontiers, the secession of many provinces (Paraguai, Alto Peru and Banda Oriental) and the political and economic conflicts faced by the regional elites because of the hegemonic vocation of Buenos Aires, thus generating permanent conditions for civil war.

The state construction, therefore, was greatly dependent on the specific political and economic conditions of each country. How the centre is shaped depends, to a large extent, on the strategy used to integrate the national elite that controls the state apparatus and also on its capacity to co-opt the peripheral elites, thus setting up the bases for a stable political pact.

This process is also associated with the structuring of the economy in the same proportion as, in function of the degree of distribution and concentration of its benefits inside the elite classes, material conditions essential to the legitimization of a state with national vocation are created. Those two processes are mutually conditioned throughout the period.

The weight of economic as political factors in the equation territorial fragmentation/belated centre, and territorial unity/precocious centre cannot be clearly stated, but their actual influence can hardly be excluded. However, if the conditions inherent to the structuring of the economy have a powerful influence, then it must be acknowledged that the political options of the elite in the transition (even with a limited margin of choice) readily affect the "centre" location, with implications upon the territorial unity. The type of the established regime, resulting from the liberal strategy adopted by the political elite when appropriating selectively the stock of ideas and institutions taken from dominant liberalism, in keeping with their political or economical interests, is also a decisive factor. Even without discussing the significant differences between the various liberal projects now under way in Latin America, it can be admitted that at that time, a British-like constitutional monarchy would move effectively to reach its objectives than a republican regime strongly influenced by American federalism.

In this perspective, it is worth mentioning that the unitary centralism of the Brazilian Empire does not fall apart until 1889, with the advent of the Republic, which was inspired in the same federalism that made Argentina (except during the "Federacao Rosista" period) an extreme case of political instability associated with the political decentralization.

Brazil, unlike Argentina, is faced with the more complex contradictions of regionalism (except for the regional rebellions during the Regency period) only during the republican period, when the major problems of national unity had already been overcome and when a stable and complex state apparatus had already been built. This difference is accounted for, according to Santos, by the very political experience of the newly independent states: "all the other Latin-American countries then independent from Spain—Brazil was one of the last colonies to become independent—had already experienced the consequences of the liberal strategy. They had become autonomous in relation to the colonial power, they had abolished slavery and they had drawn up excellent political-republican constitutions."

Nevertheless, the effects of the economical process upon the state formation cannot be overlooked. Oszlak analysing the formation of the Argentinean state recognizes that the condition of a more integrated economy, as in the Brazilian case would have added to the preservation of certain colonial institutions the possibility of producing "the cement that would amalgamate the territorially constituted society and the incipient dominant system in a national state" (Oszlak, 1982:25).

In spite of the interpenetration of political and economic variables, the comparison between the two national processes tends to show some dominance of factors of political nature. This datum, however, does not invalidate the proposition stating that "the possibilities of success to impose a natural order were conditioned both by the market situation, ruled by the group that controls exportations—port monopoly, masteony of the basic productive sector—etc. and by the capacity of some sectors of the dominant classes to consolidate a political system of domination" (Cardoso, Faleto, 1970:43).

The evident importance of this articulation remains too general and is, in fact, a kind of structural context which explains the precocious or belated appearance of the state in Latin America the differences between the Argentinean and the Brazilian processes becomes clearer if three others more specific factors which played, in our interpretation, a strategic role in the rhythm of the state construction are added: first the basic profile of the ruling class (ideological unity and political training), its role in the rupture of the colonial link and in the constitution of a state apparatus; second, the relationship between the state construction and the development, of the forms of coercive control over the society (role of the army and the militia); third, the lesser or greater degree of dissociation between the political power and the church, considering the catholic tradition of the colonizers and the influence of the religious institutions in the formation of the political system. Our hypothesis postulates that different forms of interaction of the three preceding factors with the process of construction of the political order, during the second half of the 19th century, have had a decisive influence on the establishment of the national state.

Political elites and state

The analyses of Brazilian and Argentinean elites suggest a significant difference in some characteristics that may either favour or hinder the building of the State: unity or division in the national plan; possibility of choosing specialized or non-specialized training for administrative-bureaucratic jobs; dominant profile of political-ideological values (Carvalho, 1980; Oszlak, 1982; Donghi, 1972). In this area, the contribution of Carvalho to the analysis of the imperial political elite (unfortunately with no equivalent in Argentina) makes it possible to shape the singularity of the Brazilian elite as far as Latin American patterns are concerned and to point out its political relevance during the formation of the National State.

In Brazil, the political elite that leads to independence and is responsible for the governing of the State for more than half a decade of constitutional monarchic regime, finds its originality in the statism of portuguese tradition. In this country, where the bourgeoise revolution failed to take place (and was not only delayed as in Prussia) the State becomes a hegemonial institution in society, the bureaucratic element prevailing in the elite. Whereas in England the political homogeneity of the elite was defined by its social origin, in Portugal it tends to be of ideological nature, due to the kind of political training and socialization they received (Carvalho, 1980:29-30). The most powerful element in the ideological unification of the imperial elite was the education at the beginning at the Law School of the University of Coimbra and later at the Law School in Recife and Sao Paulo, in Brazil. This education under the influence both of the Roman law and of the tradition of the Portuguese mercantilist State protects the members of the elite, as pointed out by Carvalho, from the dangers of the "French Enlightenment" (that deeply influenced the Hispano-American "criolla" elites as well as the unsuccessful emancipation attempts to gain independence from Portugal since the 18th century) training them to perform tasks inherent to the building of the State. Due to the stability of the Imperial period these characteristics can be reproduced, enabling their members, by means of long political careers (with geographic and professional mobility) to acquire an "extensive experience in government."

This statist orientation was particularly valid for those magistrates who combined the intellectual, ideological and practical elements for the job (Carvalho, 1980:69, 76 e 83).

The profile of the Brazilian political elite-unified, specialized, with juridical education and long experience in the control of the State and in civil bureaucracy-contrasted with the Argentinean political elites up to the last two decades of the 19th century. The latter, splitted and regionalized by inherent political disputes and conflicting economic interests, had not learned with the experience of a stable national government (perhaps with the exception of the "porteno" elite) and had not received a general juridical training.

This situation can be partly explained by the way the political emancipation took place, plus the burden of internal conflicts that destroy almost all traditional institution. A recent study on the formation of the Argentinean State shows that "after the colonial link was broken, it soon became evident that the Spanish domination had not furnished the basis for the development of a "criolla" political class that would be able to win, with leadership and legitimacy, the political and territorial control that had been exerted by the mother-country" (Oszlak, 1982:39). The long war finally eliminated the "peninsulars" who controlled the majority of the posts in public office, making it impossible, in contrast to the Brazilian case, to mountoun or bureaucratic elite bonded to the mother country. Consequently, in Argentina, the need to permanently mobilize the population for active service, "favoured the rise of individuals without any special training to important posts in government" (ascension through military channels), being this then the reason for "the predominance of the military over the civil 'criolla' bureaucracy" (Carvalho, 1980:89).

When the emancipatory movement (as was the case of Buenos Aires in 1810) is basically local, restricting itself to overthrow the colonial authority in its own seat and replace it for a junta, the fight for independence should be intensified.

This independence is the result, in general, of a long process of internal wars caused, on the one had, by the resistance instigated by the mother country, on the other, by the centrifugal power of the regional "caudillos." The nationalization of the Argentinean independence is the result of a long period of wars, which had as main consequence (besides the fact that it weakened the fragile statal apparatus that existed previously) the breaking up of the political solidarity between the political elites of Buenos Aires and those of the other provinces. In his study about "the formation of a ruling elite in criolla Argentina." Donghi points out that "the politics of interests that replaces the one that had been based on revolutionary solidarity, ends by disclosing, in their confused multiplicity, the world of complicity and rivalry of a reduced urban oligarchy."

He adds that the crisis of 1820, made the national project of Buenos Aires infeasible and transformed it into a group of "United Province," thus defining "the rural basis upon which to total political power would now rest" even though this "ruralization of the basis of the power" would not be "only an aspect that would affect wide areas of national life and that would consolidate the barbarization which was one of the consequences of the changes that the revolution would necessarily have to introduce" (Donghi, 1972: 388-389).

The economic and political supremacy of Buenos Aires trying to impose itself as "centre" and the active resistance of the "caudillos" rebelling for the cause of the provincial autonomy and strictly defending a "federalist" and anti-unitarian position, causes, for more than half a century, a serious problem of territorial unity and national identity, at the same time that it produces an ideological rupture in the ruling class as far as these two political projects are concerned. There was nothing in common between the unitarian institutional framework proposed by the enlightened "porteno" elites (whose liberalism was less conservative than in Brazil) and the confederation structure defended by armed leaders in the provinces. This disruptive process engenders two central components to the Agrentinean political universe: "just as the province was the creation of an independency process—a substitute for the colonial state that had disappeared—so the "caudillismo" was a substitute for the democracy associated with the independence movement," that is, "the modality that assumed locally the representation of the people, in a people unfamiliar with the democratic practice" (Oszlak, 1982: 246). In this contradiction between the centre and the periphery that was expressed by means of a long civil war (that probably influences the deep-rooted tradition of "autonomism" in Rio Grande do Sul during the Empire and the Old Republic and the radicalism of armed and electoral confrontations between Positivist—Republicans and Liberal-Federalists) (Trindade, 1979) reside two exculding conceptions of organization of a political system: "The men of Buenos Aires, observes an

Argentinean historian, held that the nation pre-existed in relation to the provinces and that the fundamental institutions existed previously to the provincial autonomy. This principle, that is rooted in the centralist enlightened group of Buenos Aires since the May Revolution, was against the Constitution of a country by means of a part that would signify the simple aggregation of heterogeneous parts, as, in general, was the intention of the federative agreements planned by the "caudillos" (Romero, 1975: 96).

The situation started to change in the direction of the formation of a national States after the Argentinean Confederation was dissolved, and at this moment there was a return to the institutional pact previous to its creation by the use of arms. Even after 1862 when there was a rupture with the "duopolio" (Confederacaoe Buenos Aires) the political elite, Oszlak says, "was very a from being a stable and strong coalition." The leadership of Buenos Aires "would dissolve in a complex process of reconstruction of the dominant coalition" and almost two decades were necessary, so that in 1889," a pact of domination relatively stable was consolidated" (Oszlak, 1982: 89-90). This paradoxical fact permits, on the one hand, to understand the parody of Oszlak, valid to Argentina of the time, according to which "The State is dead, long live the State," as the fall of the Confederation meant the beginning of a definite national organization according to the model imposed by Buenos Aires; and, on the other hand decipher the conclusion, paradoxical as well, that "there exists a tragic sign" in this formative process: "The war created the State and the State created the war." The "national unity" was created upon dissension and upon the confrontation of different peoples and political banners. The national unity has always been the price of defeat for some and the assertion of privileges for others. And the national state, institutional symbol of this unity, represented the way of transforming into routine the domination imposed by the arms" (Oszlak, 1982: 88, 89, 90 e 256).

The analysis of the role of the Brazilian elites leads us, on the contrary, to find out a greater homogeneity not only in the kind of training received, that was more adapted to bureaucratic and government tasks, but also by the existence of a political consensus between liberals and conservatives before the basic challenge that threatens the stability of the established power. This political unity of the elite is revealed since. "The turbulent periods of the consolidation of power, when various alternatives seemed to be politically feasible" and it remains practically intact in the imperial period, as the rulers "agreed upon some of the basic aspects regarding the maintenance of the unity in the country, the condemnation of military governments—either "caudillo" or absolutist—the maintenance of monarchy and, undoubtless, by the continuing slavery" (Carvalho, 1980: 107-108).

With the exception of Chile that reached "a political settling of great stability" (1829-1891) and maintained a domination system more solid than the Brazilian," there were no conditions, according to Carvalho, in Latin America to settle "stable civil governments" and to set up a political elite that would resemble the Brazilian. This difference derives, according to the author, from the fact that "the Spanish policy of creating universities in the colonies allowed the formation of local elites and prevented the effect of unification produced by Coimbra." Besides the fact that instruction was deeply tinged by religion based on the models of the Royal University of Salamanca and on the confessional University of Alcala). There was an exclusion of criollos, in great numbers, from the civil service, particularly in the Bourbon period" aiming at "preventing the continuity between colonial and independent administration" (Carvalho, 1980: 36-37).

The comparative data about the Argentinean and Brazilian political elites show clearly, besides the internal differences produced by economic contradictions and pronounced social differences mainly between Buenos Aires and the interior provinces, that the main political aim was the same for both of them. If, as viewed by the Brazilian elite, we consider that "in order to have a liberal State it is necessary first of all to have a national State" (Santos, 1978:81), we can consider that, in the Argentinean case, because of the goals of the liberal "portena" elite, the basic aim is to build a national State that will be, at the same time, a liberal State. This difference partly explains why Argentina, though delayed if compared to Brazil in the construction of a national state apparatus, creates before this country (with the rise of radicalism to power in 1916), the necessary conditions for the emergence of a liberal democratic regime. Under this view Rouguie, referring to the long process that crystallized between 1860 to 1880, interprets the project of the generation of the '80s: "only when the previous economic and political conditions are united will the ruling group finally be able to put into practice the project of modernization and transformation of the country, organized by "thinkers" of the national organization as Alberdi and Sarmiento. Inspired by the fascinating success of the United States of America that, in less than a century, thanks to the flow of men and capital from Europe, built a powerful agricultural and industrial nation, the masters of the "Argentinean utopia" intended to make their country join the group of the developed nations taking European civilization to America" (Rouquie, 1978:21-22).

The Military and the State

Besides analysing the role of the political elite in the building of the State it would be important to analyse the relationship between this fact and other forms of organization of the military group during the period of the construction of a nation-wide political power. This process that Oszlak calls "coercive penetration," implies the use of "physical violence or threats of coercion, in order to obtain obedience to the will of those who exert it and to suppress completely any resistance to authority" (Oszlak, 1982:98). In the Argentinean and Brazilian cases we should discuss not only the problem of the constitution of a permanent army after independence, but the rise of other forms of military organization as militias or national guards.

The comparisons between Brazil and the Hispano-American countries indicate some effects on the development of the military institutions deriving from the difference between the rythm in which the political emancipation took place and the consolidation of the national political structures. If, in the Brazilian case, the absence of a war of independence delays the democratization of the army, in other Latin American countries, the early Americanization of the armed forces becomes a decisive factor in making them democratic (Uricoechea, 1978a; Carvalho, 1974; Carvalho, 1980; Donghi, 1972). It seems relevant though to the logic development "undoubtedly there were armies: expeditionary, libertarian, front, guards of internal borders. There were organic projects of establishing a permanent familiar institution (. . .) however, until 1862, and during the long period of civil wars, the command of the repressive apparatus was shared by the national and the provincial governments." He adds that even during the Argentinean Confederation (1952-62), the "only military force available was the provincial army of Entre Rios" and that "the permanent disorganization of the army led to such a decrease in the number of enlisted men that in *the eve of Pavon* (*1861*) the permanent army was constituted by 3504 engaged men." These data led him to conclude that "the formation of a military force ostensibly superior to any potential coalition of the provincial forces took place only for the war of Paraguay," and consequently, "the provincial armies" started during the civil wars, emerging from the "troops mobilization and from the uprising of battalions of revolutionary armies," where "caudillismo, *marchy* and the deep-rootedness of the federal idea are phenomena intimatity linked to the formation of these local forces" Oszlak, 1982:65-98). Within this context, the concept of professionalization cannot be applied indiscriminately, because not only the wars for independence but also those against the Brazilian Empire, even though they have sped up the professionalization of the various professional armies which were far from constituting a permanent national army.

It could be even said that in the Argentinean case, the early combination between professionalization and politicization in a context of provincial armed forces was a strong obstacle, at least until 1866, to the institution of the Argentinean State.

Nevertheless, the fact that "half a century after the beginning of the emancipatory movement (. . .) the organization of the army was still an unfinished task" (Oszlak, 1982:98), does not eliminate the fact that, in the last quarter of the 19th century, a rapid expansion and professionalization of the Argentinean national army can be observed this professionalization was pushed on during the presidency of Mitre (1862-1868) at the same time as "the path to the rapid modernization of the country was opened. From this moment on the bases for "a centralized organization of national defence" are launched. The number of enlisted men that amounted to 6000 in 1864 reached the number of 8188 in 1884" (Rouquie, 1978:65). This period which was extremely demanding to the new national army, opened the many to its national (5.) Even though the Military Academy, created in 1869, had a limited effect on the recruiting of new officers, if compared to the traditional ways of joining the military career, the professionalization had been technically and corporatively accelerated, since 1873. The superior Military Academy founded in 1900, under the influence of the German army had its teaching staff completely constituted by the European officers. In 1901, draft was mandatory and fifteen years later half of the Argentinean officers had either studied in Military Academies or had joined the German troops for a period of training. These data help us to confirm the role of the army in the formation of the national State: unlike the previous phase, as Rouquie points out, "the Argentinean Army, as organized by Mitre and Sarmiento, serves to reinforce state centralization" (Rouquie, 1978:65-68).

Our contention, in synthesis, is that the Argentinean traditional army—precociously professionalized, regionalized and taking part in politics—was a factor in the delaying of the process of construction of the State. In the 80's, with the unification of the national society and its integration in the world market, the army became a decisive ally of the "national organization government," contributing to consolidate the process of political unification and centralization.

In the Brazilian case, in spite of its similarity to the Argentinean case regarding the delay in the professionalization, the relations between the army and the process of the formation of the State are different. The army, though limited in the number of enlisted men (Uricoechea, 1978a:131), will be a national institution during the Imperial period, separated from the regional power and subordinated to civil power. Only after taking part in the war of Paraguay the army begins to impose itself on the political elite and to justify its expansion and professionalization, though their rhythm and specialization are slower than the Argentinean.

During the first decade after independence the majority of the officers were of Portuguese stock, their influence decreasing in 1830 when foreigners were expelled from the army and became still weaker with the abdication of the Emperor in the following year.[6] The weakness of the army training and its small number of enlisted men forced the Emperor to hire mercenaries in order to face rebellions in the state of Pernambuco in 1824 and to fight Argentina for the occupation of the Cisplatina Province from 1825 to 1827.

The failure of the imperial army in the Prata War (that led to the independence of Uruguay in 1828), resulted in the reorganization of the army, which had its number of men fixed in to thousand and the average number of enlisted men ranging from 15 to 20 thousand, with the exception of the period of the War of Paraguay, when the numbers increased to 35 thousand in 1865 and to 85 thousand in 1869 (Schwartzman, 1982:89).

The Brazilian army, though it did not follow the democratic style of the "populist caudillos" in Argentina, experienced a significant charge in its social basis as the century progressed. Up until the first half of the century, the recruiting characteristics of the army of D. Joao VI were kept (aristocracy and nobility), social class position being much more important than professional training. From 1850 on, as rural aristocracy begins to value people with Law Schools degrees rather than those interested in pursuing the military army career, the traditional recruiting was socially looked down upon (the military schools charged no fees, while the Law Schools did). Besides the exclusion of the Portuguese officers, until 1850 the military educational system would favour the "engineering officers" over the "infantry and cavalry officers." However, when the military career starts to be professionalized, in 1880 a generalized system of promotions was established for all the arms (Schulz, 1971: 235—237; Carvalho, 1979:9—11).

It should be pointed out that during the Feijo Regency and because of the hostile attitude of the liberal politicians against the formation of a permanent army, the members of the active force were reduced to 6,000.

The reaction of the liberals was caused not only by ideological reasons ("strong armies would lead to the emergence of little Bonapartes") but by economic ("a large army would take from the production area a great number of workers") and political reasons as well ("the troop would help to bring anarchy, instead of order, for the soldiers had a clear tendency to join the people") (Carvalho, 1980:149). The principal consequence of this anti-army feeling was the creation, by Feijo, in July 1831, of the National Guard, with a wide recruiting system and based almost completely on the law of March 1831, that reorganized the National Guard in France (Castro, 1971:277).

With the return of the conservative politicians to power as a result of the explosion of the Farroupilha Revolution, in 1835, Araujo Lima, the new Regent, took the necessary steps to reorganize the armed forces. The new army had an important role to perform in the suppression of a series of regional revolts (in the provinces of Maranhao in 1840; in Minas and Sao Paulo, in 1842; in Rio Grande do Sul, 1845 and Pernambuco, 1848-49). The decade of economic development that begins in 1845 propitiates a greater preoccupation with the organization of the army, the improvement of the structure of the officers corps (1850) thus upgrading the level of instruction. Traditionally, military instruction was done at the Royal Military Academy founded by the Portuguese in 1810, which, displaying high standards of quality, was the only school of engineering in Barazil, till it was transformed into the Polytechnic School in 1874. The inconvenieonce from the military point of view was that the Academy was so interested in forming military engineers only, that it did not turn its interest to the formation of infantry and cavalry officers. From 1853 onward the military Academy of Rio Grande do Sul was structured to form infantry and cavalry officers and since 1858 the civil engineering course separated from its strictly military counterpart, starting a new institution that would function till 1904 in Rio (Praia Vermelha).[7] From that same year, the preparation for the Academy was not done only longer in civil secondary schools but was linked mainly to a network: two Superior Military Schools were founded (in Rio and Porto Alegre) besides a Military School, developing an eight-year programme of studies. Curiously, the improvement of the standards of quality of the military teaching does not follow necessarily a technical direction, as it happened in Argentina. On the one hand, Schultz recognizes that the level of the requirements for the military education "would stand out favourably, if compared to those of the civil colleges," on the other hand, Carvalho points out that "with the presence of Positivism in Military Schools, these became centres rather for the study of Mathematics, Philosophy and Letters than for the study of military subjects."[8]

It remains to be said that the influence of the foreign military missions in Brazil was different from that suffered by the Argentinean army, besides having taken place at a later date. There was a restricted period of contact with a German Mission (1906-1910), a fact which gave origin to a generation of officers called "the young Turks", however the most important role belonged to the French Mission, from 1920 on. This difference could be partly justified because the early German influence on Argentina was due to the prestige of the Bismark army, winner of Sedan, while the French army only increased its technical prestige after World War I. However, as Carvalho points out, "though limited by the Army General Staff to the *role of consultant*, french Mission had profound effects on the whole organization of the army", establishing various training coursesand special courses for the General Staff leading to the development of a "modern notion of national defence, includingthe mobilization of the economical, technical, and human resources" that had begun to be widely accepted under the influence of the "Young Turks" (Carvalho, 1974: 136-139).

This process of professionalization of the army is conducive to a progressive alteration in the level of politicization (which took place at a later date in comparison with the Argentinean case) of the Brazilian army. Little by little the young groups, by means of publications such as "O Militar" (1854), began to voice their criticism against Imperial politicies (abolition of slavery, subsidies for immigration and industry, electoral reform, modernization of transports and of the military career). However, the awakening of a critical position more structured in corporattive and political terms appears only after the war a against Paraguay, when "the officers corps emerged (. . .) with a feeling of corporative unity, a new meaning of their importance, a bitterness in relation to the civil groups and, perhaps or wider view of the world" (Schultz, 1971: 248-252). Though the question is complex, the data seem to confirm the idea that, even delayed. The politicization of the Brazilian military men was wider, that is, with more "national" turn than the Argentineans ware capable of having, submerged as they were in a confrontation which mingled national identity and a "provincial" feeling. This situuation in Argentina would have the conditions to alter itself only in the second half of the 19th century, with the beginning of the successive governments of "national organization". The politicization of the Brazilian military men can be explained, to some extent, as a result of their late professionalization.

This interpretation is confirmed by research done by Carvalho, demonstrating that, at first, "the officership became less aristocratic and more indogenous, more educated, impregnated with Positivism, had their career perfected; and they developed a higher corporative spirit',. The consequence of the process of institutionalization of the army that ended only with the Old Republic, "led the officers to a conflict with the political elite in general" and if "their ascension coincided with the decline of magistrates in the elite", the author adds, "the military were their substitutes in the end of the Empire and the beginning of the Republic. The same centralizing preoccupation and the same resistance to privatist fragmentation of power were dominant. The difference was in the political meaning of centralization (. . .). The military started to act according to the new times and with renewed strength. They gave a more urban and bourgeois content to centralization, as they fought slavery and proposed the liberation of the country from agricultural economy" (Carvalho, 1980:152-153). This effort of the army to consolidateto itself as a national organization and to fulfil a crucial role in the expansion of the national State takes place during the first experience of a Republican regime. After having taken an active part in the fall of the Empire, its monopoly in the direction of the "repressive penetration" of the State is reinforced, from 1920, with the introduction of the universal draft and the consequent removal of the National Guard as a rival organization (Caravalho, 1974-184).

However, the difference between the statization rhythm in Argentina and Brazil has to be explained as in both of them the professionalization of the national armies took place belatedly. In the Argentinean case, as it has been said, professionalization developed simultaneously to the constitution of the national power, while, in Brazil, it took place when the State had already had the bases of its domination established. Nevertheless, if the "repressive penetration" has been historically articulated with the formation of the national State how is the early building of the State in Brazil going to be understood? The answer to this question makes us take into consideration a very important repressive institution: the National Guard.

Even though in both countries "national guards" had been formed during the 19th century, the Brazilian, besides lasting longer (it was extinguished in 1866 in Argentina but only in 1922 in Brazil), started as a nationally oriented and structured institution, less submissive than the Argentinean to regional conflicts and loyalties. This difference related to the circumstances of its creation in Brazil will ultimately produce a greater impact on society than the Argentinean case. While the organization of "free men militia" intended to form a military corps that would function as an alternative to the expansion of the army and the some time, an institution that would partly substitute the permanent regular army and perform a relevant role in the extensive penetration of the State.[9] In Argentina, on the contrary, it became, first of all, a complement to the army,[10] and secondly, an administrative instrument of the State service.

The disruptive situation in Argentina forced the National Guard (though recruiting volunteers and submited to the civil power) to be more exposed to the influence of the Army than in Brazil, becoming, consequently, a more professionalized and military structured institution. The interaction between the National Guard and the Army that also takes place in Brazil partially (in the State of Rio Grande do Sul due to troops concentration because of the border with Argentina and Uruguay) does not affect the division of functions between the army (control of the borders) and the National Guard (maintaining the order inside the country against threats to the regime). As stated by the historian of the Brazilian corporation, "The National Guard—civil institution organized as an army—created as an anti-army force, become eventually and by its own rosources, a vehicle of the regular forces rehabilitation. It was a transitory solution between front-line Army and The Nation in arms (Castro, 1971:293).

Within this context, our proposition is that in Argentina the functions of the National Guard were merged with those of the army itself, hindering its potential capacity of accelerating the process of constitution of the State. The Argentinean army, as it structured itself nationally, from 1880 onward, does not face competition with the National Guard, already, extinguished, fully carrying out the monopoly of coercive force. In Brazil, in opposition, distribution of roles between the National Guard and the Army, the long duration of the first and its lesser professionalization (though in national bounds) will give in the opportunity of playing a crucial role in the process of statization.

The Brazilian National Guard fulfilled two functions, according to specialists. On the one hand, as Carvalho opines, it performed the "*liturgical administration*": "in the absence of controlling capacity of their own, the governments resorted to the free services of groups of individuals, in general land owners, in exchange for confirmation or concesssion of privileges." The author considers that "in the Brazilian situation, the liturgical association par excellence was the National Guard." Its officership was chosen from among the gentry (farmers, merchants, capitalists) and the effectives were formed by the better part of the free adult population: "From 1831 to 1873, the National Guard was responsible for almost all of the local patrolling," becoming " a powerful instrument to be used by the local chiefs to control the free and poor population."

If all the public workers of the Empire numbered, in 1877, less than 80,000 people, the National Guard had, in 1873, 6,04,080 men on active duty, rolls and 1,29,884 in the Reserve, which corresponded to 17 per cent of the free male population (Carvalho, 1979:19). On the other hand, according to Uricoechea's interpretation—"The precocious militarization of society"—the belated military professionalization is not to be taken as an absence of early militarization," because "society as a whole had been exposed to an intense process of militarization from the early days of the colonial period." This generalized influence of the military institutions was not restricted, incidentally, to the local elites, because "it penetrated most groups and classes of free men during the Imperial days, perhaps even all of them, independent of social position on status." This means that "the process of militarization of society was not just an agrarian phenomenon; it affected the urban society of those days as well." The rationale of the author, based on solid historical research, is that, as the professional army (reduced during the Empire day, except during the Paraguay war) was not prepared to act in the vast territory of the young nation, the Brazilian Empire experienced "a process of militarization of a major part of the system of positions associated to the execution of state functions and of political organization of the civil society" (Uricoechea, 1978a: 17-131).

After rejecting the conventional interpretation (which states) that process of centralization did not start until the second half of the 19th century, Urichoechea analyses its genesis in the colonial period—when the bases of a "far-reaching patrimonial bureacratic structure are established—and he claims that "it was only in the second quarter of the 19th century that conditions were ripe for the state organization to be changed in two uninstitutionalized and systematic process; Uricoechea also claims that it was the National Guard "that made the most systematic and extensive experiment of patrimonial domination in Latin America possible during the nineteenth century" (Uricoechea, 1978a: 15, 101).

The thesis of the strategic role of the militia in the construction of the State is in harmony with Birnbaun's interpretation of the French. When Birnbaun criticizes the historian of the French Revolution who "frequently neglected the careful analysis of the role of the Army in what could be called the statization of the nation" (including Tocqueville, who preoccupied with the continuity of the effort of the state construction, is silent about the role of the revolutionary armies), considers that "the construction of the state and the appearence of an Army of citizens seen intrinsically connected. The mass mobilization (la levee en masse) during the French revolution represents the essential moment of the state institutionalization" (Birnbaun, 1982:194). Following the same line of analyses Uricoechea claims the although patrimonialism had always been a component of the political organization during the colonial period it was not until the beginning of the 1830's—when the state decided to attract (through the National Guard) the private cooperation of the dominant potriarchal classes—that the state took on a more institutional and systematic from. It is exactly in this opposing and conflicting coexistence of traditional and rational forms, of patrimonialism and bureaucracy that one of the specific marks of the institutional organization of the 19th century Brazilian community lies. And, says Uricoechea, when evaluated under the historical-comparative perspective derived from the political history of our Spanish American neighbours. The process of construction of the state becomes an extraordinary achievement. "Nevertheless, what is functional to our argument is that this process is directly linked to the National Guard activity, because following Uricoechea "the contribution of the National Guard to the creation of a modern and bureaucratic state was really impressive: the relevance of the militia in the process of state construction lies among other things, in its sometimes exclusive participation in the creation and maintenance of an administrative routine of local government that was a necessary condition to the development of an institutional order beyond the limits of the patriarchal society. The continuity of the public administration that the militia made possible during two generations represents a very important factor in the process of state formation" (Uricoechea, 1978:302-305).

Church and State

Among the several factors (political elite regular army and National Guard) associated with the formation of the national state, both in Argentina and in Brazil the last one namely the Catholic Church is worth mentioning. It does not seem difficult to justify the influential weight of the Catholic Church in Latin America, if we take into account the Catholic tradition of the colonizing power, as well as the important role played by the dergymen (catholic hierarchy and low clergy) during the colonial period, even though often in conflict with the respective metropolitan centers, However influential the church may be in the development of a dominating catholic culture in Brazil and Argentina, the issue under analysis here is situated on another level, once studies on the emergence of national states have demonstrated the importance of the Catholic church in the development of the European States too (Badie-Birnbaun, 1979; Tellenbach, 1940; Strayer, 1979; Rokkan, 1975).

If we consider first that the process of dissociation and autonomization of the politician, as a privileged process of solving tensions and conflicts, originates in "cultural models characteristic of Europe", some specialists emphasize that "the most sensitive area of this dissociation is situated, without the shadow of a doubt, in the relation between the political system and the religious system." According to this analytical perspective, it would be "beyond dispute that Christianity played, in the construction and the *invention* of the State, a decisive role which grows more and more important as religion proclaimed the autonomy of the spiritual power in relation to the temporal power and then traced, in negative, the outlines of a specific political field which, in turn, had to create, little by little its own formula of legitimacy as well as a new and original way of functioning" (Badie-Birnbaum, 1979: 159-160). The analysis of the relationship between church and State in the countries under consideration, during the 19th century, does not show many contrasts—unlike the other analysed factors—even though some differences probably affecting the process of state construction do exist. Such differences can be basically reduced to the evolution of some non-converging traits in the history of catholicism in both countries.

Overlooking the fact that, during the colonial period, after a long Jesuitical influence (particularly in the Indian Reductions), the Jesuits were expelled in the second half of the 18th century, our central interest lies in the post-independence years, when some differences strike the observer. What both countries have in common is the fact that, despite the differences in the pcocess of institutionalization of the state power, both constitutions adopt a "patronage" (padroado) regime, and this make catholicism the official religion, even though allowing non-catholics the free exercise of their cult. From the days of the first Argentinean constitution, which originated in the historical Assembly, in 1813, not oniy was "the Catholic religion adopted as State religion" but even some articles of the 1812 Spanish Constitution were transcribed, prescribing that "the electors have to go to their parish (a Cathedral in the case of the Communal Provincial Assembly) where a Mass honouring the Holy Spirit will be celebrated, with the purpose of invoking the divine lights." Likewise, the Provisional Statute of 1815, which replaces the legal body then in power, rectifies the principle that the Roman, Apostolic Catholic Religion is the State religion", and the Declaration of Independence of 1818 invokes "the Eternal (who) presides over the universe." Later, when the 1924 Congress adopted the "Fundamental law", inspired in the text of the Confederation of the United States of America, the representatives (even though the monarchic idea had been definitely abandoned) commit themselves to "protecting the Catholic Religion" (Carranza, Varela e Ventura, 1978: 65, 75, 69 e 111).

With Rosas' coming to power in 1835, despite his long dictatorial period of government, the relations with the Catholic Church were not only good, but Rosas himself "benefited from the support of the Catholic Church, which was seriously jeopardized by the anticlerical liberalism of the unitarians." This support 'allowed Rosas to sanctify his regime with slogans like: "Long live the Holy Federation!—Death to the wild unitarians!" (Gerassi, 1969:20).

The Argentinean constitution of 1853, emanated from a Constitutional Congress already anticipated in San Nicolas Agreement[11] resulting from the defeat of Rosa's Army, in Monte Caseros, in February, 1852[12], evolves to a patronage regime more similar to the Brazilian model of the 1824 Monarchic Constitution.

In fact, the new Constitution "breaks with all the tradition of public statute of the Catholic Church, considering every preceding Constitution, including Alberdi with his Bases, more explicit in their recognition of the Church" (Farrell, 1976:31). The new legal situation of the Church now taking shape may be summed up in three charcteristics:

1. freedom of worship,
2. maintenance of patronage and
3. suppression of the ecelesiastic court.

The Argentinean Constituents under the doctrinal influence, of Alberdi[13] without denying the importance Christianity had actually a more royalist attitude than in the past. Alberdi tried above all to prevent the constitution organization from becoming a mere document alienated from the Argentinean tradition; in the field of the relations with the church. Alberdi claimed that "religion, the basis of all society, must be among us, a branch of education rather than of instruction. We need practising, however, that the Constitution is made within a context which allow for a broad programme of foreign immigration and this makes the representatives, still influenced by Alberdi go from a dogmatic tolerance to a civil tolerance, thus opening the possibility for a more effective exercise of the various forms of worship, out of respect for the people who professed them and to avoid moral degradation.

This issue presented in the second article of the Constitutional project raised during the debates a lively discussions of religious character (Carranza, Varela e Ventura, 1978: 182-188). In Argentina, therefore, unlike the Brazilian case, where the Church—State separation is incorporated in the 1891 Republican Constitution[15], the "patronage" (padronado) regime is maintained without changes until the rules of the game were altered during the Peron Government.

In Brazil, the Constitution of the Empire, besides invoking God's name in the preamble ("Dom Pedro Primeiro, by God's grace and unanimous acclamation of the peoples, Constitutional Emperor and Perpetual Defender of Brazil") aa well as the "Very Holy Trinity," prescribes in the Fifth Article: "The Roman Catholic Apostolic Religion will continue as the Religion of the Empire. All the other denominations will be allowed their private worship, in buildings destined for this specific purpose, with no external features of a temple" (Almeida, 1967: 3-4). The freedom of worship guaranteed by theConstitution will, however, be limited, in its practice by later regulations, of the Civil and Criminal Code, by parliamentary regulations, by College statutes and so on, which implies bestowing to the Catholic religion "the privilege of official religion, mandatorily to be respected by all,"[17] according to the chapter in the Constitution dealing with "General regulations and guarantees of the civil and political rights of the Brazilian citizens": "No citizen shall be persecuted for religious reasons, so long as he shows respect towards the State and does not offend the public morality" (Art 179, para 5) (Barros, 1971: 319; Almeida, 1967: 40).

However, the officialization of the Catholic Church in the form of a quasi-monopoly of cult and of the strong privileges which it had at its own disposal in public and political functions, did not necessarily generate consensus at the level of institutional relations with the State. During the Brazilian Imperial period, heir of the royalist tradition of the Portuguese State, the system of patrodage ended up by causing conflicts between the two powers throught the 19th century, the main consequence of which would be the separation between church and State with the fall of the monarchy in 1889. These conflicts originated to a great degree, in the limitations imposed by the State upon the autonomy of action of the Church, especially requiring the Imperial approval for the "decrees of the Councils and Apostolic Letters and whichever other ecclesiatical Constitutions" (Art 102, para 14), as well as the power to "Indict bishops and provide for ecclesiastical benefits" (Art 102, para 2). However, matters of the borderline between the spiritual and temporal fields[18] caused frequent conflicts which would lead towards the "religious question," leading to justice, in 1872, two Brazilian bishops (D. Vidal e D. Macedo). The situation worsened because, despite the weight of the Church, we know that, while the country declared itself Catholic in its majority the country was on the margin of the Roman faith" (Barros, 1971: 321). On the other hand, if a process of Romanization had been started since Gregory XVI and Pices IX, that is to say, a process of centralizing the hierarchical power of the Church returning to the bishops a degree of authority over the clergy unknown since the colonial period (Moura e Almeida, 1977: 328), up to that period the situation was rather different. Actually, "the national clergy, from the days of the Marquis of Pombal on the religious question, was not distinguished with rare exceptions, by any demonstrations of orthodoxy" (Barros, 1971: 321). Unlike the plitical elite, which had been marked by the conservative liberalism of the Law School they attended, the clergy in general had absorbed the liberal and republican ideals of the Seminar of Olinda (which explains its involvement in the revolutionary movements of 1817 and 1824). The main consequence of that situation, and of the fact that during the Empire the priests were paid by the State, was that of producing paradoxically, an attitude as royalists as that of the political elite. A typical example of such an attitude was the movement in favour of the abolition of religious celibacy led by Feijo (a priest who would latter become an Imperial Regent), who proposed its extinction by the General Assembly of the Empire.[20]

The most interesting aspect in the logics of our argument, however, results from the relationship between the clergy, as a bureaucratic section linked to the State, and its articulation with the process of its formation. On the one had, the dependence of the State reduces the clergy to the role and to the situation of civil service (Moura, Almeida 1978: 325). On the other, the clergy constitutes an administrative body, widely spread throughout the country, whose members (the parish priests) play religious, administrative and political roles (Carvalho, 1979: 11). Before the arrival of the Ultramontanism in Brazil, in the last quarter of the 19th century, the ecclesiastical bureaucracy was a branch of the public service. Despite the active participation of priests in the emancipatory rebellions of the Colonial Period, and that throughout the reign of Pedro I and until the end of the Regency Period the clergy had been deeply involved in politics, it is important to note that the loyalty resulting from patronage ended up by the originating a supplementary controlling tool of the State over Society. This specificity of the role of the clergy in Brazil (which disappears with the advent of the Republic and which probably does not receive as much political weight in Argentina) allows Carvalho to admit that due to the low cost of its maintenance by the State[21] "the recognition of the great social power of the clergy made the government reluctant to abandon its control which was also an inexpensive administrative resource . . ." (Carvalho, 1979: 12).

NOTES

1. The analysis of the articulation of both countries appears in the following articles: Trindade (1984a) *Bases of the Brazilian Democracy: liberal logics and authoritarian praxis (1822/1945)*, Paris

(mimeo) and Trindade (1984b), *State penetration and liberal dynamics (1880/1930): comparative aspects of the Argentinean and Brazilian political process* (in progress). For another analytical perspective see Alimonda's important contribution (1982).

2. The first historian to oppose the thesis of the feudal character of the hereditary "*capitanias*" was Simosen (1944), who opposed the traditional theses expounded by Ribeiro and others. More recently, Furtado (1954) admits the possibility of "feudalism" as a result of the regression caused by the atrophy of the rural economy.

3. Concerning the influence of the University of Coimbra over the formation of the Brazilian elite, see Carvalho, chapter 3, "Unification of the elite: an island of scholars" (Carvalho, 1980: 51-72).

4. Carvalho refers, in his book "*The Construction of Order*," to a passage of the classical "*History of the Univrersity of Coimbria in its relations with the Portuguese public instruction*" by Teofilo Braga, emphasizing the importance of the Bolognese juridical influence over Portugal: "The jurists were the theoretical organizers of this monarchic dictatorship; the transformation of the feudal regime under D. Joao I takes place due to the preponderance of Joao das Regras, a jurist of the Bolognese school" (Carvalho, 1980-20).

5. The Argentinean army was involved in 107 revolutions and 90 combats, nearly five thousand people having perished (Oszlak, 1982:102).

6. Schultz indicates that "D. Pedro was congenial with the Portuguese, appointing several of them to high political and military posts. But in 1830 the Emperor was forced to dismiss all foreigners from the army. His abdication in the following year, followed by his death in 1834, weakened the Portuguese Faction considerably, though there is evidence that the Portuguese had a greater power of permanence than it is Generally imagined" (Schültz, 1971:238).

7. According to Schultz, "Army officers should attend each of these institutes for one year, while artillery officers and General Staff officers should attend the Central School for three years, and then go to Praia Vermelha; Army Engineers attended each of the schools for four and two years respectively. No military student attended the Central School during the war against Paraguay, and it was transformed into the Escola Politecnica (Polytechnical School) in 1876 (Schulz, 19:246).

8. According to Carvalho, unlike the Army, the Navy "was not invaded by Positivism, a fact which lessened the political involvement of the students" and in the curriculum of the Naval School there was "an excess of mathematical and theoretical teaching, "*whereas* the changes made by Benjamin Constant in the Praia Vermelha School, it "even had a discipline in Sociology" (Carvalho, 1974:135). Concerning the Navy, Paula notes its role in the consolidation of the national unity, preventing Brazil from "fragmenting itself into a series of republics—as it happened in the Spanish America—had it not been for its unifying action (Paula, 1971:272).

9. Historians distinguish three distinct phases in the National Guard: "The first phase, roughly, that of the minority, from 1831 until the reformation of the Law in 1850, when the corporation, as a large popular body, acted directly and intensely in the campaign for national pacification. The second phase, which comprehended the reign of Pedro II, from 1850 to 1889, was characterized by the beginning of the aristocratization of its governing bodies, to become, later, and electing militia—a corps of officers without soldiers. Finally, in the third phase, the republican, will "witness the absorption of the civil militia by the army, as a second line corps, continuing as such until its very end in 1922 (Castro, 1971;274).

10. "La intercambibilidad de las fuerzas (v.g ejercito de linea o guardias nacionales) y de los destinos militares se convertio en un hecho cotidiano, sobretodo a partir de la declaracion de guerra al Paraguay (. . .). Hasta 1876, la Guardia Nacional servio de importante refuerzo del ejercito regular, ante contingencies que colocabam a este en situacion precaria. Al constituirse practicamente en una institucion permanente, su existencia posibilitoy acelero la capacidad del estado en todo ambito territorial (. . .). Antes de desaparecer la Guardia Nacional continuaria siendo movilizada, no solo para custodiar las fronteras interiores sino ademas, para sufocar nuevas rebliones" (Oszlak, 1982:103-105).

11. The Agreement "acknowledges the 1831 Federal Pact as "Ley Fundamental" and establishes the bases for the convocation of the Constitutional Congress, which will have to meet in August in the city of Santa Fe." Even though it had been anticipated that "each Province will have two representatives. elected in accordance with the laws in power in the Province;" the absence of Buenos Aires (in tentative secession), does not prevent the Constitution from being approved by majority of ballots (Carranza, Varela e Ventura, 1978:173).

12. The military power which defeated "the tyrant Rosas" was made up of a coalition of "portenhos," Brazilian and Uruguayan soldiers, and his own party supporters (Gerassi, (1968:21).

13. Alberdi's contribution was decisive, particularly his "Bases y puntos de partida para la organization politica de la Republica Argentina" (Alberdi, 1966).

14. The provincial constitution of Buenos Aires said in the first article: "Buenos Aires es un estado con el libre ejercicio de su soberania interior y exterior, mientras no lo delegue expressamente en un gobierno federal" (Oszlak, 1982:74).

15. The 1891 Republican Constitution, article 72, paragraph 7, embraces the principle that "no cult or church will receive state subvention, neither will it maintain relations of dependency or alliance with either the State or Federal Governments."

16. It is interesting to observe, despite the similarities of the Church/State relations in Brazil and Argentina, the differences of the educational systems between both the two countries. In Brazil, the State allows the church to control the teaching structure (in the secondary level, for example, except for the D. Pedro II School, the teaching is predominantly in the hands of the Jesuit priests); in Argentina, conversely, a lay experience in teaching is developed, under the leadership of the liberal Buenos Aires elite and, most of all, through Sarmiento's educational action.

17. As Barros observes, "freedom of conscience, though theoretically supported in article 179 of the Empire Constitution, was limited not only by the criminal code and the College Statutes, but by the Constitution itself through article 5 and the third paragraph of article 95, which deny those who "do not profess the State religion "the right to become representatives of the people" (Barros, 1971:329).

18. "As if the spiritual realm were not as historical as the temporal realm as Barros rightfully points out" (Barros, 1971:320).

19. In his classical work "*A Cultura Brasileira*" (*The Brazilian Culture*), Fernando Azevedo notes that, if the theorists of the encyclopaedists came to constitute the ideology of these political movements in Brazil, or at last contributed to give them the one of the times, they did not grow enough to fracture the unity to of the culture or to

strongly colour education with its tendency, whose maximum expression within the domains of education was the Seminar of Olinda, created in 1798 and founded in 1800 by Bishop Azeredo Coutinho (Azevedo, 1943:325).

20. The publication in which this point of view is aired, and is supported by a good number of liberal clergymen, was entitled "*Demonstracao de necessidade da abolicao do celibato clerical pela Assembleia Geral do Brasil e da sua legitima competencia nesta materia*" ("*Demonstration of the necessity of the abolition of priest celibacy by the General Assembly of Brazil and of its legitimate competence in this matter*").

21. See also in "*A Constrncao da Ordem*" ("*The Construction of Order*"), Chapter 7, "Judges, Priests and Soldiers: The meances of order" (Carvalho, 1980: 133-153).

REFERENCES

1. *Alberdi*, Juan Bautista (1966), *Bases y puntos de partida para la organization politica de la Republica Argentina*, Buenos Aires, Eudeba.

2. *Alimonda*, Hector (1982), *Paz y Administration—Ordem e Progresso*: expansao exportadora e formas politicas na Argentina (1860-1916) e no Brasil (1889-1930), Sao Paulo, Tese de Doutorado em Ciencia Politica, Universidade de Sao Paulo.

3. *Almeida*, Fernando H. Mendes de (1967), *Constituicoes do Brasil*, Sao Paulo, Ed. Saraiva.

4. *Anderson*, Perry (1978), *L'Etat Absolutiste* (L'Europe de l'Ouest), I, Paris, Maspero.

5. *Azevedo*, Fernando de (1943), *A Cultura Brasileira*, Rio de Janeiro, Institute Brasileiro de Geografia e Estatistica.

6. *Badie*, Bertrand and *Birnbaum*, Pierre (1979), *Sociologie de l'Etat*, Paris, Grasset.

7. *Barros*, Roque S.M. de (1971), Vida Religiosa e A Questao Religiosa, in Holanda, Sergio Buarque de, org.. *Historia Geral da Civilizacao Brasileira*, (O Brasil Monarquico), Tomo II, vol. 4, Sao Paulo, Difel.

8. *Birnbaum*, Pierre (1982), *Lo Logique de l'Etat*, Paris, Fayard.

9. *Cardoso*, Fernando Henrique and Faletto, Enzo (1970), *Dependencia y desarrollo en America Latina*, Cidade do Mexico, Siglo Veinte Uno Editores.

10. *Carranza*, A.R.; *Varela*, A.R.; *Ventura*, E. (1978), *Manual de Historia Politica y Constitutional Argentina* (*1776-1976*), Buenos Aires, AZ Editores.

11. *Carvalho*, Jose Murilo de (1974), As Forcas Armadas na Primeira Republica: o poder desestabilizador, *Cadernos do Departamento de Ciencia Politica*, (1), Belo Horizonte, p. 111-188.

12. *Carvalho*, Jose Murilo de (1979), A burocracia imperial: a dialetica da ambiguidade, *Revista Dados*, Instituto Universitario de Pesquisas do Rio de Janeiro, (21), Rio de Janeiro, p. 7-31.

13. *Carvalho*, Jose Murilo de (1980), *A construcao da ordem*: a elite politica imperial, Rio de Janeiro, Editora Campus.

14. *Casiello*, J. (1948), *Iglesia y Estado*, Buenos Aires, Toblet.

15. *Castro*, Jeanne B. de (1971). A Guarda Nacional, in Holanda, Sergio Buarque de, org., *Historia Geral da Civilizacao Brasileira* (O Brasil Monarquico), Tomo II, vol. 4, Sao Paulo, Difel.

16. *Cintra*, Antonio Octavio (1974), A Politica Tradicional Brasileira: uma interpretacao das relacoes entre o centro e a periferia, p. 30-77, in Balan, Jorge, org., *Centro e periferia no desenvolvimento brasileiro*, Sao Paulo, Difel.

17. *Donghi*, Tulio Halperin (1972), *Revolucion y guerra*: for macion de una elite dirigente en la Argentina criolla, Buenos Aires, Siglo Veinte Uno Editores.

18. *Duarte*, Nestor (1939), *Ordem privada e organizacao politica nacional*, Sao Paulo, Editora Nacional.

19. *Faoro*, Raymundo (1948), *Os Donos do Poder—Formacao do patronato politico brasileiro*, Porto Alegre, Editora Globo.

20. *Farrell*, Gerardo T. (1976), *Iglesia y pueblo en Argentina (1860/1974)*, Buenos Aires, Ed. Patria Grande.

21. *Furtado*, Celso (1976), *La Economia Latinoamericana*: una sintesis desde la conquista iberica hasta la revolucion cubana, Santiago do Chile, Editorial Universitaria.

22. *Gerassi*, Maryusa N. (1968), *Los Nacionalistas*, Buenos Aires, Ed. Jorge Alvarez.

23. *Holanda*, Sergio Buarque de (1969), *Raizes do Brasil*, Sao Paulo, Editora Brasiliense.

24. *Iglesias*, Francisco (1976), Revisao de Raymundo Faoro, *Cadernos do Departamento de Ciencia Politica*, (3), UFMG Belo Horizonte, p. 123-142.

25. *Moura*, Sergio L. de and *Almeida*, Maria G. de (1977), A Igreja na Primeira Republica, in Fausto, Boris, org., *Historia Geral da Civilizacao Brasileira* (Sociedade e Instituicoes—1889/1930), Tomo III, vol. 2, Sao Paulo, Difel.

26. *O'Donnell*, Guillermo (1980), *Modernization and Burocratic-Authoritarianism*: Studies in South-America, Berckeley, Berckeley University Press.

27. *Oszlak*, Oscar (1982), *La formacion del Estado argentino*, Buenos Aires, Editorial de Belgrano.

28. *Paula*, Euripedes Simoes de (1971), A Marinha, In Holanda, Sergio Buarque de, org., *Historia Geral da Civilizacao Brasileira* (O Brasil Monarquico), Tomo II, vol. 4, Sao Paulo, Difel.

29. *Reis*, Fabio Wanderley (1984a), Solidariedade, interesses e desenvolvimento politico, *Cadernos do Departamento de Ciencia Politica*, (1), Belo Horizonte, p. 5-58.

30. *Reis*, Fabio Wanderley (1974b), Brasil: Estado e Sociedade em perspectiva, *Cadernos do Departamento de Ciencia Politica*, (2), Belo Horizonte, p. 35-74.

31. *Rokkan*, Stein (1975), Dimensions of State Formation and Nation building: a possible paradigm for research on variations within Europe, in Tilly, Charles, org., *Formation of National States in Westhern Europe*, Princeton, Princeton, University Press.

32. *Romero*, Jose Luis (1975), *Las ideas politicas en Argentina*, Buenos Aires, Fondo de Cultura Economica.

33. *Romero*, Jose Luis (1979), *Breve historia de la Argentina*, Buenos Aires, Editorial CREA.

34. *Rouquie*, Alain (1978), *Pouvoir militaire et societe politique en Republique Argentine*, Paris, Presses de la FNSP.

35. *Santos*, Wanderley Guilherme dos (1978), *Ordem burguesa e liberalismo politico*, Sao Paulo, Editora Duas Cidades.

36. *Schultz*, John (1971), O Exercito e o Imperio, In Holanda, Sergio Buarque de org., *Historia Geral da Civilizacao Brasileira* (O Brasil Monarquico), Tomo II, vol. 4, Sao Paulo, Difel.

37. *Schwartzman*, Simon; (1970). Representacao e Cooptacao Politica no Brasil *Revista Dados*, (7), Rio de Janeiro, Instituto Universitario de Pesquisas do Rio de Janeiro.

38. *Schwartzman*, Simon; *Reis*, Fabio Wanderley; Cardoso, Fernando Henrique (1977), As eleicoes e o problema institucional, *Revista Dados*, (14), Rio de Janeiro, Instituto Universitario de Pesquisas do Rio de Janeiro.

39. *Schwartzman*, Simon (1982), *Bases do Autoritarismo Brasileiro*, Rio de Janeiro, Editora Campus.

40. *Strayer*, Joseph R. (1979), *Les origines medievales de l'Etat moderne*, Paris, Payot.

41. *Tellenbach*, Gerd (1940), *Church, State and Christian Society at the time of the investiture conflict*, Oxford.

42. *Trindade* Helgio (1979), Aspectos politicos do sistema partidario riograndense (1882-1937), in: *RS*: *Economia e Politica*, Porto Alegre, Ed. Mercado Aberto.

43. *Trindade*, Helgio (1984a), *Bases da democracia brasileira*: logica liberal e praxis autoritaria (1882/1945), Paris, (mimeo).

44. *Trindade*, Helgio (1984b), *Penetracao do Estado e dinamica liberal (1880/1930)*: aspectos comparativos do processo politico argentino e brasileiro, Porto Alegre, (em elaboracao).

45. *Uricoechea*, Fernando (1978a), *O Minotauro Imperial*, Sao Paulo, Difel.

46. *Uricoechea*, Fernando (1978b), Coroneis e burocratas no Brasil Imperial: cronica analitica de uma sintese histnrica, p. 201-225, in Nunes, Edson de Oliveira, org., *A Aventura Sociologica*, Rio de Janeiro, Zahar.

5

SOME THOUGHTS ON INDIAN DEMOCRACY

MAX JEAN ZINS

Is the coexistence, within a given society, of massive underdevelopment, and of a parliamentary, multi—party form of democracy, a paradox? This question is often asked in relation to India by many observers who have dwelled upon contemporary Indian politics. Its terms, however, do not apply specifically to Indian reality but refer rather to European history. Fundamentally it contains a series of postulates derived from a comparative approach, which takes the democratic regimes of the industrialised West as its "model." Seen in this perspective, the question poses a dilemma only if and when one accepts these postulates. The reasoning here is based on a comparison between two types of historical sequences. The first pertains to the advanced European countries where the disappearance of feudalism and the advent of industrialisation *prefigured* the growth and the development of political parties and of the parliamentary system. In this historical process, the democratic experiment, initially reserved to a small elite, could be gradually diffused to the entire society. The inceasing participation of the masses in the political process strengthened the legitimacy and the efficacity of the political system and firmly entrenched democracy in civil society.

The second type of sequence concerns the so called third world countries. In their case, the economic "take-off" has to occur in the framework of a social environment where the democratic tradition is *as yet in its infancy*. More often than not, the rulers here are constrained, for the attainment of modernisation ideals, to impose "hard", not to say dictatorial, forms of State domination on the society. Following this sequential differentiation, we arrive schematically at the following propositions: a democratic policy would be the natural lot of industrialised countries, whereas dictatorship would fit in more with the underdeveloped world. Or putting it differently: democracy would be a luxury which the "third world" cannot offer itself. India would in this case appear to be the rare, if not the only example of a state which is, at the same time, very poor and democratic. It would thus be a deviant case, and it would be in the interest of all the developing countries to meditate upon the example of the greatest democracy in the world, which could furnish, in Rajni Kothari's terminology a "model" enabling them to avoid the perilous path of right of left adventurism.[1]

This type of reasoning, employed with some variations by different authors[2], raises a series of questions; for example, what type of democracy is one referring to in India and in the West? What is its class content, if any? Why restrict the definition of democracy to its political dimension alone, and what is worse, often to only one of its forms, the party system? How many countries in the world, including in Europe, conform to the Western "model?" Can it be affirmed that democracy is widening in scope in the West? Is there any interrelationship between the success of the democratic experience in these countries and their long history of colonial exploitation whose victims constitute today's disherited nations? The list of questions could be infinitely prolonged with the risk of making us drift away from our subject. It is wiser and more pertinent in the framework of our paper to restrain ourselves as strictly as possible to the Indian case. I would, however, like to specify that I use democracy as a sufficiently extensive and abstract concept, which takes on different concrete forms, in different countries and at different historical moments. Here, democracy implies the participation of the largest possible section of the masses in determining and fashioning their future under a given set of conditions. Having thus qualified it, I will attempt (1) to explore certain factors which could explain, at least partially, its existence in a certain, specific form in India (multi-party and parliamentary system) (2) to analyse the functioning of one aspect of this democratic regime (the political system); (3) and lastly, to explore certain trends in its evolution during the recent years.

I

Three series of factors have undoubtedly contributed towards shaping the face of Indian parliamentary democracy. The first is related to the socio-economic level that India had reached at Independence (1947), largely, if not solely, due to the development of big private capital; the second to the vast influence then exercized by urban middle classes; the third to the exclusion of the peasantry from central decision-making centres in New Delhi during the first two decades of independence.

1. The first aspect, often masked under "third world" generalizations, needs to be briefly recalled. New Delhi's image in the West is so much linked to underdevelopment and poverty[3], that one tends to forget that today India is the world's tenth industrial power, and that as far back as in 1947, it had already attained a non-negligible level of development. As a matter of fact, India at independence offers a rare example of a decolonised country where indigenous capital is capable of successfully competing with that of the "metropolis."[4] It will not be far-fetched to assert that in 1947, the major part of capital invested in India belonged to the Indian bourgeoisie. Its development was without doubt hindered by colonial constraints.[5] But the big business circles in India represented at the end of the World War II a very influential social strata. Certain "big families" were, besides, associated with the

independance movement, were close to the leadership of the Congress Party, and financed it partially.[6] In 1947, the industrial and financial circles belonging quasi-exclusively to the big bourgeoisie (the small and medium scale modern business enterprises *have* not as yet surfaced) are sufficiently powerful to envisage the independent, "self-reliant" development of Indian economy. At the same time, they are conscious of their structural weakness[7] and aware that they need, for safeguarding their domestic market and their developing potential, the "threshold" support of the public sector and of a planified economy.[8] Due to these characteristics, this social segment will figure at the heart of the post-War problems concerning India's development strategy: how to preserve and then enhance national independance. The big business thus will be capable of playing in national life an essential role, totally incomensurate with its feeble numerical strength.[9]

To put it briefly, at independance, India could boast of a bourgeoisie, who was not *compradore* and had all the means of exercising a "determining" political influence. This phenomennon simply reveals that India's political independance, in a way, only followed and consecrated its economic independence. From this point of view, the sequential differentiation referred to above would not be valid. The Indian case would not be an exception, but would rather confirm the historical process specific to industrialised European countries. In other words, the Indain situation is not really paradoxical: a part of its economic development preceded the establishment of its political system, the latter in this sense was not an artificial "graft" on a totally backward socio-economic environment. Under these conditions, the Indian elite gradually gained the experience of a parliamentary democracy, which, designed to meet its interests, firmly established its national legitimacy. Parallely, it hastened the country's autonomous economic growth. To fully understand India's smooth adaptation to a democratic, it has system to be remembered that the Congress Party existed since 1885, that in 1947 it was already 52 years old, that its foundation coincided, at just a few years interval, with that of the Labour Party in Great Britain, of the two major American parties, and of the Radical Party in France.

2. The second aspect deals with the influence of urban middle classes, which is again a distinctive feature of Indian socio-political life.[10] Right from 1947, they are capable of exercising a great deal of influence on the level of the Central-State apparatus as well as on the Congress Party. They find in Jawaharlal Nehru their representative and exercise their hegemony on the Indian/State through their preponderant influence within the Indian Parliament, which became the main arena for their political bouts and allowed them to establish links with the rural masses during different legislative election campaigns.

One of the reasons for this has been highlighted, amongst other authors, by Charles Bettelheim.[11] He has underlined, besides their numerical importance in relation to other *stratas* of the Indian society their way of life and their socio-urban environment, which moulded and oriented their ideological approach towards what the Congress Party called in its Avadi Resolution (1954) the "socialistic pattern" of society. The urban intelligentsia in the large sense, broader adorned with the mantle of its participation in the independence movement, could naturally consider itself as called upon to preside over the nation's destiny, the more so in the absence of any other competing or rival social strata issued either from the peasantry the small industry or commerce, capable of playing this role.

A second series of reasons has been advanced by Rajni Kothari, who emphasises certain aspects of Pan-Indian culture to explain the ability of the Indian political elite originating from urban middle classes to exercise its functions of leadership on the civil society.[12] For instance, Kothari notes the fundamental cohesion of Indian society based essentially on a stream of cultural identities, of a religious essence (*i.e.*, "a political" in Kothari's terminology). He further notes its absence of identification with a given political order. It is thus "*mainly to lack of previous political references that the new political order could gain legitimacy in Indian society in so brief a period.*" Due to this factor, the "political centre" formed at the level of the central State by this new elite, which gradually assumed the reins of power of the "real" country from the end of last century onwards, enjoys a great deal of autonomy in relation to the society. In other words: (1) the deep and traditional divide of Indian society in two words—one political (at the centre) and the other a political (at the local and intermediary levels of different cultural identities); (2) and the just as deep and traditional cohesion of this society would explain why: (a) the new political elite could impose on the country new values (parliamentary system universal suffrage . . .); and (b) could diffuse them in society without overthrowing the social order, so profoundly marked by the cultural values of Hinduism An additional reason for this to happen, according to Kothari, is the fact that this tradition culture of the Indian civil society was permeable to new political values which germinated in the West and were adopted by the Indian elite.

The two series of arguments advanced by Kothari and Bettelheim are fundamentally different in nature: one is derived from the marxist approach and focuses on the class-analysis of Indian society; the other is essentially cultural in scope and effect; if not based on its class basis. But both note the determining influence exercised on the State by the new Indian elite derived from urban middle *stratas*, which was capable of giving orientation the young nation's socio-economic policies.

3. The marginalisation of the peasantry is in sharp contrast to the role played by the above mentioned social *stratas*. If one were really to look for a paradox in India, would it not be in the fact that in a massive peasant society, the peasants are massively excluded from central power and from decision-making centres called upon to define and implement the nation's economic strategy? (This would, of course, be major difference with the other "giant" peasant State of the world, China).

In the immediate post-Independance years, the fate of the peasantry was sealed the day the Constituent Assembly decided to *confer to* the provincial Legislative Assemblies the *competence for* agrarian reforms. This question was thus taken out of the purview of the central parliament, which had emerged as the most radicalised institution at independance, thanks to its domination by the progressive urban intelligentsia. The landed vested interests represented in Vidhan Sabha could thus safeguard their privileges But givin their very nature (they belonged to economic formations which werc gradually disappearing), they could not contribute in any significant way to the development strategy being defined by the new Indian elite at the central level, and were, thus, largely excluded from this new post-war problematic of Independent India.

At the same time, the Constituent Assembly's decision seriously obstructed and slowed down the pace of implementation of land reforms[13] permitting the emergence of dynamic rich, middle and small capitalist farmers. It was only from the mid-sixties onwards that the gradual, regionally disparate expansion of agricultural capitalism produced a new type of leadership, directly interested in the political and economic stakes being debated at the level of central power.[14] Its appearance on the political stage coincides with all sorts of pressures which begin to weigh on India's political and parliamentary systems. It can be deduced from this phenomenon that without this Constituent Assembly's decision of the Indian, democracy would probably not have assumed the same from as it did in the subsequent period.

In the same manner, it can be asserted that the political marginalisation of the greater segment of the rural world, the mass of poor peasants and lendless agricultural labourers, accounts for the successful *practice* of Indian democracy in its specific form. The history of independent India offers just one example of peasant struggle which mobilised the poor, landless peasant in whole rigion: this was the Telengana guerilla struggle spearheaded by the Communist Party of India from 1946 to 1951 in the State of Andhra Pradesh. There in "liberated" zones, was introduced a mode of social and political organization radically different from that conceived and put into practice by the Congress Party.[15] This rebellion, as is well known, was taken serious note by India's central leadership and suppressed with extreme brutality.

Without entering into the debate as to the necessity of a revolutionary social transformation of Indian society which would be a "*realistic precondition for breaking down the social barriers to development*",[16] I would just like to summarize a series of reasons which together explain the exclusion of the peasantry as a whole from the main, dynamic political stream after 1947. These reason are partly *historical*: while mobilising the Indian masses in order to provide the Indian National Congress with the social support needed to fight the British, Mahatma Gandhi took utmost care to control the peasantry (one could add, as much as the working class) and to undermine its volition for social change.[17] They are partly *cultural*: the consensus and cohesion of civil society and its separation with "political" society noted by Kothari can explain the *perennity* of backward values with hamper the breakdown of social relationship in the countryside. They are partly *social*: the state of utter misery and subjugation to which million of men and women are still confined in India is one element (amongst others) limiting the role of the peasantry. They are also partly *economic* in nature: a number of authors have shown the slow growth and the difficulties in the process of capitalist development of agriculture, this development remaining still incomlete, and what is worse, perhaps incapable of being ever completed.[18] All these factors, difficult to expand upon within the scope of this paper, account for the absence of any dynamic political role played by peasantry in 1947, with a few exceptions in some parts of the country.

II

Parliamentary democracy in India would note be what it is without a very original political system, whose characteristics have been aptly described in a number of works. In fact, it is a system, usually called the "Congress System," which gave to the Indian democracy its subtance and colour for at least 30 years (1947-1977). To explain its mode of functioning, I will outline two of its essential features: the "bloc in power"[19] and the one dominant party system.[20]

The bloc in power: The Indian State since independance

represents the interests of a "bloc in power" formed by politically dominant social stratas and classes (their dominance) being determined by a number of different factors, economic, sociological, historical, psychological, etc). Its twin main components, of more or less equivalent strength, represent those very stratas whose preponderant role was *evoked* in the beginning of this paper: 1) the big industrial, financial and commercial bourgeoisie (whose interests in the wake of independance are linked, even though paradoxically, to landed feudal or semi feudal elements);2) the urban middle stratas, disposing a network of personal and ideological relationship in the countryside, their most influential faction being constituted by the urban intelligentsia in the 50's and the 60's. As far as reciproca relationships between different components of the block are concerned, they can be summarized as follows: it is more than a mere alliance; out it is not a total merger.

It is more than a mere alliance inasmuch as the internal contradictions of the bloc are always less acute than those which oppose it to the classes/stratas it dominates. The minimum threshold of unity which the bloc maintains enables it to control and exercise state power for the benefit of all its components. In other words, the compromises entailed in the search for a common denominator permitting this "threshold unity" (this common denominator reflects the basic consensus of the block) are compensated by the vital advantages derived by the very fact of the bloc's existence (the years 1947-1950 are the most fascinating illustrations the working relationships within the bloc and its paramount importance for all its components).

Buu it is not a total merger. At the same time, the bloc does not realize the complete merger/fusion of the different stratas composing it, as their divergent interests tend sometimes to be antagonistic. Moreover, the different components do not have the same status/position within the bloc: one faction leads the bloc, the other aspires to and struggles for its leadership. This is because the coexistence of two components within the bloc does not imply that State power is shared equally by them, even if there is a certain sharing of influence as far as the different organisms of State apparatus are concerned. However, at the highest level, the unity of State power is symbolised by the existence of a Prime Minister who is the real "decision-maker" on all vital issues.[21] Frictions and tensions within the bloc crystallize over this question of the bloc's leadership, a question which is directly related to the competition for State power and which fundamentally structures the political game in India.

Given the heterogeneous composition of the bloc, its leadership has to be very flexible. Given the nature of the bloc, its leading component can only safeguard its leading position within the bloc if at the same time it takes into account (and satisfies to a large extent) the aspirations of its "dominated" partner/ally and allows the latter to express its demands. The fulfilment of this last requirement is essential for the unity of the bloc. If we call this flexible mode of functioning "hegemony," then we can say that the bloc is composed of an "hegemonic" element and of a "non-hegemonic" element. In this sense, the notion of hegemony is antithetical to the notion of monopoly, of dictat, and a fortiori a dictatorship. If we admit that the hegemonic component must, to remain hegemonic, recognize the legitimacy of the non-hegemonic element, it follows that political hegemony can only be established on the basis of a democratic functioning of the political game.

As far as the hegemonic and non-hegemonic components are concerned, I have worked on the hypothesis that the big bourgeoisie constitutes the non-hegemonic component of the bloc, whereas the middle stratas compose the hegemonic component. One determining factor in establishing their hegemony has been their capacity to draw towards them—and by extension towards the bloc—the support of a very large majority of Indian masses. The hegemonic/democratic mode of direction of the bloc has probably been decisive in regard to this majority support. Nehru is perhaps the best example amongst Congress leaders, who could mobilise public opinion in his favour, in favour of his policies and win the necessary amount of electoral support to assure/guarantee, via a stable majority in parliament, the political stability of the bloc. No other leader, *assimilated* by public opinion to the big business or to big landed interests could have fulfilled this role. It is because the big bourgeoisie was aware of Nehru's value in this respect and also because it knew that Nehru would do nothing to endanger the global domination of the bloc that it got reconciled to his leadership (be it with varying degrees depending upon the period and the groups concerned). As long as the major portion of the Indian masses stayed within the *ideological, political* and *cultural* stream of the Congress, the middle stratas could retain their hegemony. It is only when the Congress party began to suffer from electoral erosion (beginning 60's) that the big bourgeoisie started to wonder if the time was not ripe for it to take over the bloc's direction.

The one-dominant party system: From the very first years of independence, the rules of the political game in India were chalked out. Unlike the Western democracies where the struggle for State-power is articulated by the existence and interplay of different competitive parties, in India this struggle passes within one-dominant party, which covered by itself and for a very long period, practically the whole political space, During 30 years of Congress Raj (1947-1977), the struggle for political hegemony is led within the Congress itself. Rather than a political party, the Congress can best be described, during this period, as a vast "sub-field" within the larger political field. It was the main arena for the struggle for State-power. In other words, the power-struggle was led mainly *inside* the party in power.

The rules of the "Congress system" are derived from this reality. Thus, in the Centre, it is the dominant party, sufficiently united to avoid splitterings and a break-up, sufficiently heterogeneous to absorb the greater portion of the power-struggle in the country. Factions within it play the role of quasi-parties. This is clearly evident from the crisis of 1950-51 and of 1960, when the party's right wing openly challenged the other wing led by the Prime Minister. On the periphery are small opposition parties whose role (as far as the functions of the "system" are concerned) is limited to putting pressure from outside on the Congress factions with whom they have political affinities. The smooth functioning of this system requires a great deal of flexibility within the Congress (absence of rigid party discipline, for instance), as well as between the Congress and the opposition parties on the periphery.

Within the Congress, any attempt by one faction to impose stringent rules of discipline, would be equivalent to usurping or occupying for its exclusive benefit the quasi-totality of the political space. This would be contrary to the very principle of hegemonic direction of the bloc, which implied, as we said earlier, taking into account the legitimate interests of the minority non-hegemonic component.

As far as the relations between the Congress and the opposition parties are concerned, they function on the following pattern:

The support of opposition groups sought by the Congress factions and the different demands/pressures exercised by the former on the latter, aim at modifying the relations of force between the two components of the bloc in power. On the one hand, the Congress group representing the non-hegemonic component tends to retract from compromises that it is constantly obliged to make with the hegemonic component. To do this it needs and looks for the support of conservative parties on the periphery of Congress. Inversely, the most determined elements of the hegemonic component try to limit the extent of compromises made by the party leadership with the right wing. In this task, they look for help from the left parties/groups—indeed sometimes even from the Communist parties if the stakes are high enough (if there is a risk of shifting of the internal balance of the bloc, for instance). The best example of these alignments is the crisis of 1969, when all the political forces in the country were divided along a left/right axis (left parties and leading Congress faction versus right parties and conservative and "oppositional" Congress faction).

Thus, the Congressmen situated on both extremes tend to weigh as much as possible on the centre of the party in order to turn the scale as much as possible in its favour. This mechanism, finally and constantly, brings back the whole game towards the centre of the party: every time the Congress leadership swerved away, whether too much on the right or too much on the left of the centre of gravity, it risked discontenting one of its factions, and perhaps risked provoking a split as well. The smooth functioning of this system required thus a twin condition: on the one hand a sufficiently solid consensus within the Party to allow the expression of intra party competition/rivalry, and on the other a great deal of flexibility within the Congress (absence of rigid party discipline, for instance) as well as between it and the opposition parties on the periphery.

From this intricate and contradictory game, originated the competing forms of Indian democracy after 1947. This democracy, because of the existence of a dominant party, has sometimes been qualified as imperfect or incomplete, or distorted. However, nothing seems less exact when one examines the mechanisms of the Congress system. Political democracy was one of the fundamental rules of Indian political life, but this democratic functioning referred solely to the flexible mode of relations established within the different components of the bolc. This specificity of Indian democracy provides the basis for understanding the gradual deterioration and the present crisis of the political system in India.

III

For the last 15 years (which shows that the movement is not contingent), signs of a profound political evolution of India's political and parliamentary systems have emerged. On the political level, the crisis of 1969 already reflected a certain fracture of the Congress system. The tensions aroused by this conflict, its public character and the Congress split which ensued, indicated that the previously well-oiled mechanisms of the system were getting warped. The consensus within the Congress was no longer as strong; the search for a compromise between the right and the left wings of the party was proving to be more delicate; the leadership of the Prime Minister (who personifies at the highest level the leadership of the "bloc in power") was increasingly contested; forcing her to impose her decisions in an inflexible manner on that faction of her party, openly and virulently criticizing her political options (in 1969, the nationalisation of banks constituted the economic substance of differences opposing the two wings of the party). Under these conditions, safeguarding the unity of the party, while at the same time, reasserting the primacy of the Prime Minister became a more and more difficult exercise. Similar problems arose for maintaining the centre/centre-left orientation of her policies. As a corollary, relations between the Congress party and the opposition were also evolving; the left parties were more directly supporting the Prime Minister and the left, centre/left factions of the Congress; the conservative parties were adopting the same attitude vis-a-vis the Deputy-Prime Minister and Congress's right wing. In fact, it can be claimed that, due to these new rigidities, the problem of the very viability of the Congress system was posed before the country right from the 1969 split onwards.

Even though the Prime Minister succeeded in avoiding a major split along a left-right axis (just a splinter group decided to leave the Congress) and tried, after the crisis, to reestablish the party's balance at the centre, the increasing diffiulties of this enterprise gradually came to the fore. With the sharpening of social contradictions from 1972 ownards, it became particularly hard to realize. Confronted with growing internal dissensions, the Prime Minister had recourse to more and more "disciplinary" actions, which further warped the Congress machine.[22] Accusations of dictatiorship were slowly, from 1973-74 onwards, launched against her and massively employed by the strong opposition movements, which, grouped around J.P. Narayan, raised the banner of the defence of democracy. The backbone of this socially heterogeneous movement was formed by conservative parties.[23] In 1975, the situation had deteriorated to such an extent that the Prime Minister had no choice except, either to resign or to keep herself in power through forms of leadership totally antithetical to the "hegemonic" mode of functioning which was in vogue since 1974. This was to lead to the proclamation of Emergency, which represents perhaps one of the rare examples of a "centrist dictatorship" in the world. It aimed at perpetuating at all costs (i.e., at the cost of authoritarianism) the hegomony of the middle stratas within the bloc in power.

This phenomenon gave its distinct colour to the Emergency and explains its specific features, of a more complex nature than is generally admitted. The Emergency engendered, through its distortions of the rules of the political game, the emergence of new seats of power which were virtually dictatorial and congenial to the overthrow of "hegemony" from within the new regime instaured.[24]

The authoritarian mode of relations imposed within the bloc by its hegemonic component lead, in the system's logic, to the loss of its political legitimacy, as a prelude to the loss of its hegemony. The greatly enfeebled role *assigned* to Parliament during the Emergency, the curtailement of freedom of speech, and, generally speaking, the perversion of all rules or regulations which permitted the free expression of political dissent, political competition and power strugggle within the Congress system, reinforced the very forces who from 1947 onwards, were struggling to gain the leadership of the bloc in power. The Emergency, in fact, provided them with the very institutional tools needed to reverse the hegemony from within the bloc. It signed the death certificate of the Congreas system: Since 1977, India's political life has, in fact, been structured around a new party system.

A similar evolution was under way at the level of parliamentary institutions. Since the 60's, minority views from within the Congress itself[25] had begun to question its efficacity. from 1969 onwards, the hypothesis of a change in India's constitutional regime surfaced openly. It is important to recall here that the immediate, conjuctnral cause for the 1969 crisis was the election for the post of President of the Indian Republic. The official Congress candidate, imposed by its right wing Sanjiva Reddy), against the wishes of Indira Gandhi, then Prime Minister, was narrowly defeated by the "unofficial." Congress candidate V.V. Giri supported by the latter. The victory of

Sanjiva Reddy would probably have meant much more than the defeat of Indira Gandhi. It would have weakened the position of the Prime Minister in relation to that of the President who, it should be remembered, is constitutionally doted with enormous power. In India, the Prime Minister's stature as the sole Chief of the Executive derives from political practice or custom based on the British model and on the existence of a majority party in Parliament. Under new political circumstances, it is envisageable to imagine a move away from the parliamentary to the presidential form of government without a radical overhual of the constitution. This was a distinct possibility in 1969, in case of the Prime Minister's defeat (during his electoral campaing, Sanjiva Reddy had promised not to ratify the ordinance on the nationalisation of banks). A few years later, (1975-77), the Emergency revealed the extent of this drive against the parliamentary system. A draft bill for modifying the constitution was even circulated officially within the Congress party, but one ignores to this day Mrs Gandhi's opinion or sentiment in this respect. These attempts, moreover, coincided with the parallel undermining of parliament's role in controlling the actions of the Prime Minister, from the mid-sixties onwards. This development became so potent that certain authors even started talking about the "Prime Ministerial regime."[26] The conjunction of this dual phenomenon (the demand for a presidential regime and the "presidentialist" character of the Prime Minister's increased powers or prerogatives) probably lead to the proposal mooted during the Emergency to elect the Prime Minister through direct, universal sufferage.

All these trends, manifestation of increasing tensions within Indian politics, found a parallel in evolutions within the bloc in power. To begin with, the big bourgeoisie increased its influence over the period in relation to the other social strata, both on the social and political level. It is precisely within this social segment that one finds the partisans of a presidential system.[27] As for the middle strates, there has been drastic, qualitative and quantitative change in its composition. The urban intelligentsia no longer occupies the same place as it did in national life; its weight has correspondingly diminished. At the same time, new and upcoming elements of the "modern" small and middle bourgeoisie have made tremendous progress with the economic boom manifest in independent India. This is the case of the small and middle entrepreneurs totally absent from the social landscape in 1947. This is also the case of the rich peasantry, even though enormous regional and intraregional disparities subsist in the agricultural field. The rich capitalist farmer is now becoming a dominant factor in political life. For the first time in India history, a faction of the peasantry has a voice in decisions concerning the national strategy of development: it concerns with the pricing of oil, of manure, production of machine-tools and implements for agricultural purposes, with the nationalisation of banks, which allowed it to bypass the village usurers. It is investing in agriculture and is increasingly implicated in politics.

This evolution in the bloc's composition is reflected in many aspects of the new social reality. For instance, the erosion of the influence exercised by the intelligentsia together with the growth of the big bourgeoisie and the new capitalist agricultural groups, leads to a dilution of the Congress ideological discourse, even though this at one time cemented Congress unity and constituted the rallying point of the Indian masses to Congress politics/policies. Another example would be the spurt in tensions provoked by the increasing regionalism, which could be partly a manifestation of the eruption of the dynamic segment of the peasantry in political life, its political and cultural horizon being limited by the frontiers of its province.

At the same time, the "bloc's" domination on civil society is increasingly contested. This is linked to the modification of social relations, brought about by the crystallisation of class identities.[28] The resultant augumentation of tensions and conflicts is not without an impact on political life, even though this does not imply an "automatic radicalisation" as there is no mechanical link between cause and effect in this field. As a matter of fact, most of the new forms of conflict and contestation are expressed through the traditional social channels which are sometimes "perverted" for the purpose. All this occurs in the context of simultaneous economic growth and of increasing poverty (every month, the number of births exceeds that of deaths by about a million; hals of this humber is condemned to live below the poverty line). The worsening of inequalities had led certain authors to talk about the existence of "two nation" in India, one rich and educated, the other poor and illiterate.[29] This new socio-economic setting calls for a redefinition of relationships within the different components of the bloc in power and between the bloc and the society (since about a decade, a search is on for a new balance within the bloc, but this equilibrium stays fluid and unstable).

In this context, the question of the modification of India's political and institutional regime becomes relveant. For instance, how will it face the new tensions appering in the country: tensions linked to regionalism, more frequent social and political violence, resurgence of new forms of communal clashes, etc? What is the spectrum of ideologies it will adopt to ensure its future? The "socialist" discourse employed by the urban inteligentsia during the 50's and the 60's no longer hold any appeal. Can it now be adequately replaced by the intelligentsia's new themes related to the defence of individual liberties and democratic rights, themes which originated as a reaction to the Emergency, but which do not directly pose the problem of State power, and are limited to contesting India's socio-economic reality[30]? Given that the very idea of national independence, central to govenmental ideology and policies since 1947, is losing its driving force under the onslaught of new doctrines (new for India) of liberalism, will the quasi-official Congress slogan "Preparing India for the 21st century" be dynamic enough to mobilise the requisite national energy? Will the search for cultural and religious identities affecting India's different communities, notably the Hindu majority, be a source of greater unity of greater disruption? Even more important is the interrogation as to the evolution of India's capitalist path of developmet: can it, under the domestic and international constraints, reach the later stages of modern economic growth leading to a highly developed capitalist society? In other words, till what point or degree is the new economic strategy of Rajiv

Gandhi "*capable of engendering rapid growth over an economically significant period*"[31]? These are questions for which no easy or even definite answers are as yet available, but which will determine the future of Indian democracy.

NOTES

1. Kothari R. (1970), *Politics in India,* Orient Longman, New Delhi, p. 424.

2. See for instance: Subrahmanyam K. (Feb. 1984), "Safeguarding the Republic," in *Strategic Analysis* (New Delhi), pp. 873-890.

3. This image, in its caricatural form, is expressed in the French novel *Parias,* of P. Bruchner (Seuil Paris,).

4. See Kidron M. (1966), *Foreign Investments in India,* Oxford Univ. Press, London.

5. Levkovsky A.I. (1966), *Capitalism in India: Basic Trends in its Development,* People's Publ. House Delhi,

6. See Birla G.D., *In the Shadow of the Mahatma: a Personal Memoir,* Orient Longman, New Delhi, 1953; Tata J.R.D., *Keynote,* Tata Press, Bombay, 1986; Kochanek S., *Business and Politics in India,* Univ. of California Press, Berkeley, 1974, p. 230.

7. Bettelheim C. (1962), *L'Inde independante,* A. Colin, Paris, pp. 98-119.

8. The "Bombay Plan," formulated by a group of big Indian industrialists in 1944, proposed the introduction of the public sector in Indian economy in order to compensate the structural weakness of the private sector, enabling thus the latter to solidify its foundations and protect the domestic market against foreign competition.

9. Hazari R.K. (1966), *The structure of the Corporate Private Sector: a Study of Concentration, Ownership and Control,* Asia Publ. House, Bombay.

10. Mishra B.B. (1961), *The Indian Middle Classes: their growth in Modern Times*, Oxford Univ. Press, London.

11. Bettelheim C., *L'Inde Independante, op. cit.*, pp. 126-134.

12. Kothari R. (1985), "Democratic et non-Democratie" in *E prit* (Paris) 2, pp. 18-30. See also Kothari R,. *Politics in India, op. cit.*, pp. 160.

13. For a first approach to land reforms in India, see Thorner D., *The Agrarian Prospect in India*, Univ. Press, Delhi, 1956.

14. Thorner D., "The Emergence of Capitalist Agriculture in India" in *The Statesman* (Calcutta), 1, 2, 3, 4 Nov. 1967.

15. Sundarayya P., *Telengana People's Struggle and its Lesson*, Communist Party of India (Marxist) Publ., Calcutta, 1972.; Seshadri K., *Rural Unrest in India*, Intellectual Publ. House, New Delhi, 1983; Desai A.R., *Peasant Struggle in India*, Oxford Univ. Press, Bombay, 1979.

16. Frankel F.R. (1984), *India's Political Economy 1947-1977; the Gradual Revolution*, Oxford Univ. Press, Bombay,

17. Dutt R. Palme (1979), *India Today*, Manisha, Calcutta,

18. See, Patnaik U., "The Agrarian Question and Development of Capitalism in India" in *Economic and Political Weekly* (Bombay), 3 Dec.

19. I am using here a concept evolved by Poulantzas N., *Pouvoir Politique et Classes sociales*, Maspero, Paris, 1972, vol. 2, pp. 59-70.

20. On this notion. see Kothari R., "The Congress System in India" in *Asian Survey* (Berkeley), 4 (12), 1964, and Morris-Jones W.H., "Dominance and Dissent: their Inter-relations in the Indian Party" in *Government and Opposition* (London), August-Oct. 1966.

21. For those who would question the plausibility of sharing State power at the top-most level, see the correspondence of Sardar V. Patel (Dputy Prime Minister) and his differences with Jawaharlal Nehru: *Sardar Patel's Correspondence*, Navjivan Press. Ahmedabad, 1971-1974, vel. 6, p. 9 et sq.

22. Cf. Hart H.C. (ed.) (1976), *Indira Gandhi's India: a Political System Reappraised*, Westview Press, Boulder, Colerado, (chap. 4: Kochanek S.A., Mrs. Gandhi's Pyramid: the New Congress, pp. 93-124).

23. Shah G., "Revolution, Reform or Protest? A study of the Bihar Movement" in *Economic and Political Weekly*" (Bombay), 9.16, 23 April, 1977.

24. Cf. Zins M.J, *Le regime d'urgence Indien 1975-1977): de l'Hegemoni a la Dictature*, Etude conduite pour le Centre d'Analyse Comparee des Systemes Politiques, Univ. de Paris I, Paris. Photostat copy, Centre d'Etudes de I'Inde et de I'Asie du Sud, Paris.

25. Zins M.J., *La Question du Regime Presidentiel en Inde*, Dossiers de l'Institut des Sciences Juridiques du Developpement, Univ. de Paris, 1981.

26. Jain H.M., "Changing Role of the Prime Minister: Is India Moving towards a Prime-Minsterial System?" in *Journal of the Society for Study of State Governments*, April-Sept. 1973.

27. See Kochanek S., *Business and Politics in India, op. cit.* p. 33.

28. See on this point the publications of Andre Beteille.

29. Kothari R., "Flight into the 21st Century" in *Times of India* (New Delhi), 27 April, 1986.

30. Cf. the publications of these two organisations: People's Union for Democratic Rights (PUDR) and People's Union for Civil Liberties (PUCL). See also Lokayan Bulletin (New Delhi).

31. Patnaik P., "New Turn in Economic Policy" in *Economic and Political Weekly* (Bombay), 7 June, 1986.

6

THREE PATHS TO DEMOCRACY IN THIRD WORLD COUNTRIES?

DIRK BERG-SCHLOSSER

The analysis of the conditions of democracy is one of the central concerns of political science. Some authors even defined the discipline as "the science of democracy" (cf., Berg-Schlosser/Maier/Stammen 1985a-17f.). Under closer scrutiny, this subject turned out to be a very complex one, relating to "micro," "meso"—and "macro"—levels of analysis, distinct historical and cultural settings, international factors, normative concerns, etc.

In a "Third World" context, for a considerable period of time rather simplistic concepts of unilinear processes of "modernization" and "social mobilization", based on social and economic factors like urbanization, alphabetization, industrialization etc., tended to dominate (for a more detailed criticism, see Berg-Schlosser 1985b). More sophisticated analyses and actual political developments, however, soon dispelled any premature optimisms. A concentration on external factors of development and underdevelopment then re-oriented the attention of many political scientists in this field (for a detailed discussion, see also Migdal 1983).

Only in recent years have there been renewed attempts to take a more comprehensive look at the internal and external, economic and political factors of "development" and democratization. This paper will discuss some of these conditions on a "macro-quantitative "basis, *i.e.*, it will be restrained to the overall "system"—level of analysis and will employ, at least in rough approximations, available quantifiable strata. In doing so, it shares of course, the many limitations of such an approach (cf., *e.g.*, Ragin 1981). But even under these restrictions, a more differentiated pattern of social conditions and historical developments of more democratic forms of government in Third World countries emerges, which can refute or raise some hypotheses for more detailed research and more thorough comparative case studies, extending over other levels of analysis as well, in the future.

For the purpose of this analysis, those Third World countries have been selected which demonstrate at least a certain degree of "democratization" and whose political systems have been relatively stable for the greater part of the 1960-1980 period (for which sufficient comparative and longitudinal data have now become available).

At first, a number of general factors such as size, regional and historical conditions, social structures and the socio-economic forces mentioned above will be discussed. In this context, some of the overly sweeping generalizations alluded to can be refuted. Only as a second step will an attempt at additional multi-variate analyses be made which can lead to a series of more concrete hypotheses concerning the joint impact of these factors and the various "paths" of democratization they may reflect.

I. Analytical steps

1. The selection of cases

Any selection of cases will necessarily depend on the operational definition of "democracy" and the period of time under observation. If one applies a relatively stringent criterion as does Lijphart (1984) (based on scores of 1 or 2 on the "Freedom House" index of political rights for the year 1980 cf. Gastil,

1981) and if one chooses a relatively long period of time ("continuously democratic since the Second World War"), then not a single Third World state will be found to figure among the world's 21 stable democracies. Lijphart himself, however, notes that at least India (since 1947) and Costa Rica (since 1948) must be considered as marginal cases (p. 39). Powell (1981) gives a list of 28 democracies for the period 1967-1976 and ten of these belong to the Third World. Only five of them, though, proved to be stable during the following years (Jamaica, Sri Lanka and Venezuela in addition to Costa Rica and India). Dahl (1971) adds Trinidad/Tobago, Colombia, the Dominican Republic and Malaysia (the latter under the designation of "near-polyarchies" on the basis of data by Banks and Textor (1963). This corresponds approximately to Rustow's (1967) list which also includes Mexico. A certain consensus thus seems to exist for the 1960 to 1975 period with respect to the above-mentioned ten countries. Other democratic states listed by these authors (such as Chile, Lebanon, the Philippines, Turkey and Uruguay) no longer belong to this category as a result of decisive system changes. Dahl also notes that certain "micro-states" would still have to be added to his enumeration (p. 247). In addition, the newly independent African states do not figure in any of the lists cited here.

For the present purpose of comprehending the conditions of democracy in a relatively broad sense, a rather "generous" concept of democracy has been adopted. Starting with Dahl's definition of polyarchy (*i.e.*, "a regime in which opportunities for public contestation are available to the great bulk of the population," (p. 202), "nearpolyarchic" and "semi-competitive" systems have been included which have proven to be stable for more than ten years up to 1980 (for the use of the term "semi-competitive" cf., *e.g.*, Hermet 1978, the exact operationalization of the concept under consideration is further discussed in Berg-Schlosser 1984a). In this way, countries with intermediate levels of "inclusiveness?" (as for example Colombia) and with certain restrictions on "competitiveness" (as for example Mexico or Kenya)—these are Dahl's two main dimensions—are taken into consideration. Such a procedure reflects the main interest of this analysis which is less oriented towards gradual variations among the cases considered than towards the operationalization of a relatively broad but qualitatively distinct concept pertaining to a basically open and pluralistic type of system. The use of such a concept enables the addition of a further twelve coutries to the list of near democratic states: the Bahamas, Barbados, Botswana, Egypt, Fiji, Kenya, the Maldive Islands, Mauritius, Papua-New Guinea, Senegal and Singapore. Some of these countries, however, must be considered as marginal cases. The Bahamas and Papua-New Guinea, for example, only became formally independent during the 1970's but had possessed largely autonomous governments before that time. Egypt presents the case of a fairly gradual change from more authoritarian to "semi-competitive" structures.

2. Analysis of basic conditions

(*a*) *Size*

One basic condition of democratic political systems is their very size. In "classical" terms, from Aristotle to Rousseau, democracy in the sense of a direct and active participation in the process of public decision-making by a large number of citizens only appeared feasible in small-scale political units which allowed for personal face-to-face communication by the population at large. Even a contemporary micro-state like Luxemburg with its approximately 0.4 million inhabitants would have been huge compared, for example, to the ancient Greek or late medieval Italian city states. Madison, however, already realized that "the introduction of the representative principle into modern Governments . . . has shown the practicability of popular governments in a larger sphere, and that the enlargement of the sphere was a cure for many of the evils inseparable from the popular forms in small communities" (quoted from Padover 1965, p. 9). In fact, all contemporary democracies, whether in the Third World or elsewhere, are of the predominantly representative type at national level. It nonetheless seems striking that a large proportion of the cases considered here consists of micro-states, with less than one million inhabitants. Of the 103 Third World countries which had been independent for more than ten years in 1980, 13, *i.e.*, 12.6 per cent were micro-states, whereas the corresponding figure for the Third World democracies is six out 22, *i.e.*, 27 per cent. A further seven of the countries considered here—again a rather high proportion of the total—have less than ten million inhabitants. Conversely, among the states with a population ranging between 10 and 100 million which constitute the majority world-wide only a relatively small percentage is made up by democracies in the Third World. Nonetheless, the "greatest democracy on earth," India, with its approximately 700 million inhabitants is included in our sample.

It is not possible to go beyond this purely descriptive observation at the moment. Relationships between the size of a country and its degree of democratization consist of a large variety of political—cultural factors, detailed institutional regulations etc., which cannot be adequately considered on the basis of the material at hand. As Dahl and Tufte (1973) note, there may be specific reasons which govern functioning of both small-scale socially relatively homogeneous and large-scale often highly hetrogeneous democracies under their respective conditions. Among the latter, however, federative institutional set-ups such as exist, for example, in India seem to prevail. As for the rest, Dahl and Tufte's coclusion appears plausible: "Citizens of democratic countries face a rather similar situation whatever the size of their country: they needs to adapt democratic ideas and institutions to the fact that different problems are best met by units of different sizes" (p. 135).

(*b*) *Regional and historical conditions*

Another factor which at present can only be discussed in a very broad sense is that of specific regional conditions. Of the countries under consideration, nine belong to the Latin American region in the widest sense of the term, seven are in Asia five in Africa and one is in the Middle East (see Table 1). Among the nine "Latin American" states, however, four (the Bahamas,

Barbados, Jamaica and Trinidad/Tobago) are previous British colonies. In geographical terms we thus have a fairly wide distribution in almost all Third World regions exept for a distinct underrepresentation of the Middle East (including the North African States) where, in addition, the "consociational" system of Lebanon proved a very special case until 1975.

A cultural factor of possible relevance in this regard is the dominance of one or several religious communities in the countries under examination (see Table 1, column 7). Here again we arrive at a fairly broad distribution: five countries are predominantly Catholic, four Protestant, two have mixed Christian populations, four Islamic, one Hindu, one Buddhist and in one traditional local beliefs prevail. In four countries no single religious group predominates. The potentially positive or negative effects which membership in these communities has upon the democratic character of attitudes and beliefs cannot be dealt with here. This would require a careful analysis of the doctrines peculiar to each religious group also including important minority positions at least within the Protestant, Catholic and Muslim communities. Furthermore, the actual distribution of religious affiliations in contemporary societies and its relationship to political behaviour would have to be assessed in a representative manner. All this, of course, is clearly beyond the scope of this paper and there have been very few studies on the subject (if., *e.g.*, Berg—Schlosser 1986b), let alone systematic comparative analyses published thus far. It is probably only in the remaining traditional monarchies that we can still speak of a relatively close link between religious belief and the existing political order. As Huntington (1966) convincingly demonstrates, however, even they are subject to an increasing crisis of legitimacy as a result of strong secularizing pressures.

In view of these findings, the effect of political-cultural formation by the former colonial power appears to be more important than religious affiliation. In this respect a very clear picture emerges: 16 of the 22 states under consideration had been colonized by the British, 5 formerly belonged to the Spanish colonial empire and only a single country (Senegal) was part of the French overseas territories. Despite failures in a variety of other cases, the "Westminster" model is the system which seems to have taken root most often in the context of our sample. Included among these countries with Westminster-style systems are, however, the vast majority of small and micro-states (12 out of 14); only Egypt, India, Kenya and Malaysia have larger population. As important as the kind of colonial rule is of course the duration of that experience. India is the country with the most extended period of colonial rule while Egypt has had the briefs experience in this regard. Those cuntries which belonged to the former Spanish empire, an entity without any democratic traditions of its own, established their present political institutions at a much later stage. Senegal proves a special case among the former french colonies since four local communities had acquired democratic rights at a relatively early moment in the country's colonial history (cf.,e.g., Ziemer 1984). Rustow's (1970) argument that certain "background conditions" and a later "habituation" phase are necessary for democratic institutions and behaviour to take hold thus seems to find some support here. The kind of colonial utilization ("mise en valeur") these countries experienced has also led to a certain differentiation (see Table 1,column 4). Some of the smaller states (such as Gambia, Singapore and Trinidad/Tobago) were colonized primarily for strategic or trading purposes. Botswana is another special case, having been founded as a labor reserve for neighbouring South Africa. For the majority of countries, however, the utilization of mineral or agrarian raw materials provided the predominant motive for colonization. In countries where mining was a major activity (for example in Mexico and, to a certain extent, in Malaysia), this led to the relatively early emergence of a industrial labour force with various attempts at union organization (cf.,e.g., Tetzlaff 1977). The consequences for the social structure which the utilization of agrarian raw materials entailed depended on the predominant form of organization adopted by the agricultural enterprises. In some countries (Barbados, Jamaica, Sri Lanka and a few others) large-scale plantations were set up by foreign companies which employed indigenous labourers or, as was sometimes the case in former times, imported slaves. In other instances (e.g., in Colombia, Kenya and Venezuela) immigrant settlers employed indigenous labour on large-scale farms under a variety of tenant and wage relationships. A third pattern consisted in the commercialisation of peasant agriculture as, for example, in parts of Papua-New Guinea, Senegal, Egypt (under the special conditions of an originally "hydraulic" society, cf. Wittfogel 1957, and later Kenya. The case of Costa Rica which was characterized by the immigration of small and middle-level farmers is a typical for the greater part of Latin America. In the following paragraphs these aspects will be further considered in terms of various hypotheses relating to overall social structural configurations.

(*c*) *Factors relating to the social structure*:

In this context we must first distinguish between "horizontal" and vertical" differentiation (cf.,e.g., Blau 1976). Horizontal structures consist of nominally different groups which can be distinguished according to certain objectifiable ethnic, racial, religious or similar "communalistic" criteria (for a closer definition c.f.,e.g. Melson and Wolpe 1970). Our sample includes societies which are differentiated along several of these cleavages. Predominant among the ethnically fractionalized countries are the African and Asian States (see Table 2, column 1) with India, Kenya, Senegal and Malaysia as the most notable examples.

Latin American countries, on the other hand, reveal horizontal stratification pattern which in most cases reflect the racial origin of their inhabitants. In many instances, however, only gradual distinctions between different types of racial mixtures (e.g. mestizos mulattos, etc.) prove socially relevant. Costa Rica is the sole case in our sample with a predominantly European immigrant population. Except for the remaining portions of the indigenous Indio population, all Latin American countries show themselves to be basically homogenous in linguistic terms as well. Of the Middle Eastern states discussed here, only Egypt has a population which is similarly homogenous in ethnic and linguistic terms. This distribution thus does not differ in any significant way from the mean for all Third World countries.

In terms of conflict-group theory, however, not only overall fractionalization indices, but also the concrete proportions between group sizes are of interest (cf.,e.g. Nordlinger 1972). In this regard, the most intensive conflicts are likely to occur in "bicommunal" societies in which one group exercises a distinct and continuous hegemony (cf.,Milne 1981). Of the countries under consideration here, Sri Lanka definitely fits into this category as its extended history of ethnic strife between the Sinhalese majority and the Tamil minority demonstrates. Botswana, Mauritius and Singapore also possess single dominant ethnic groups (see Table 1, column 8). Under such circumstances "consociational" political solutions appear the most feasible (see McRae 1974, Lijphart 1977). In Botswana and Singapore indications of such a pattern within the hegemonic party are discernible. An almost equal balance between the largest ethnic groups without either being dominant is found in Fiji, Malaysia and Trinidad/Tobago. In Gambia, Kenya and Senegal a limited number of middle size groups exist. In these instances as well (for example in Fiji, Kenya and Malaysia) certain elements of consociationalism can be observed. The remaining countries are very highly fractionalized in ethnic terms, have a predominantly mixed population which is gradually distinguished or are largely homogenous. In all these cases competitive or semi-competitive forms of political contestation (the latter being the case in Egypt and in Mexico) prevail (see Table 4, column 6).

In some of the states included on our sample, ethnic and linguistic differentiation coincides with religious differentiation. In cases where a plurality of traditional indigenous religious beliefs prevail (as in Botswana or among parts of the population in Kenya and Papua New Guinea) this does not constitute an additional element of conflict. In other cases where ethnic differentiation coincides with membership in one of the larger religious communities (as in India, Malaysia, Mauritius or Sri Lanka), a reinforcement of existing cleavages may result. Conflicts may then take quite fundamental and often violent forms. Conversely, the cross-cutting of ethnic and religious groups on a large scale and a high level of overall religious fractionalization may lead to a reduction of actual conflicts (see Table 2, column 2). This applies, for example, to Gambia, Kenya and Trinidad/Tobago. A further group of countries is characterized by conflict between elements of the population with a strong attachment to religion (or in some cases a fundamentalist orientation) and their more secularized counterparts. This can be observed in Egypt, Senegal and to a certain extent in some Latin American states.

On a vertical plane, differentiation within the social structure takes place mainly in three contexts with respect to political power, economic privilege and—as a "subjective" element—prestige (cf.,e.g. Lenski 1966). In some of the countries considered here, pre colonial traditions still play a certain role in this regard. One basic form of traditional social and political structures can be found in socalled "acephalous" societies (cf.,e.g. Middleton and Tait 1958).

Here, common decisions arrived at in a collective manner on a largely eqalitarian basis for example by "councils of elders" or similar institution. The level of participation in these decision making processes which the members of the communities at large used to enjoy was considerable. Economic differentiation between individual families or persons remained small under the conditions of a subsistence economy with largely eqalitarain rights of land usage. "Prestige" was usually an individual matter and did not lead to permanent differentiation between social groups. Among the countries contained in our sample, acephalous communities existed in Fiji, Kenya and Papua-New Guinea. Such communities could also be found in other countries among minority groups. As a number of more recent studies show, these traditions can still be of relevance to contemporary processes of democratic decision-making (Barkan and Okumu 1978, Berg-Schlosser 1982 b).

In the majority of cases considered here, however, hierarchically structured societies prevailed. These were either based on feudal modes of production (as in large parts of India and

Malaysia) or on an "African" mode of production (Cocquery-Vidrovitch 1976) with communalistic property but individual land usage rights (as, for example, in Botswana and Senegal). The "Asian" mode of production with state property rights, the bureaucratic administration of irrigation agriculture and peasant usage rights was a very special case (see Sofri 1969) and, in our sample, restricted to the "hydraulic" society of Egypt. In many instances, such socio-economic relationships found further expression on the spiritual and cosmological level. To a certain extent and in certain areas these expressions persist up to the present day even though the original mode of production has undergone significant changes in the meantime. This is the case, for example, in some of the hierarchically organized traditional societies in Africa which vest "chiefs" and kings with certain spiritual functions and applies also to areas influenced by Islam and Hinduism (see, for example, Paden 1973, Packard 1981).

In Latin America hardly any pre-colonial traditions persist as a result of the widespread eradication and, in some areas, elimination of the indigenous population. Only where segments of the original India societies survive (as, to a certain extent, in Colombia and Mexico) may various cultural influences still prove relevant. These influences, however, generally possess very little significance at the present-day national level. On the contrary, contemporary agrarian structures have to the largest extent been moulded by the "neo-feudalistic" relationships characteristic of the latifundios which were introduced under Spanish and Portuguese colonial rule (see, for example Caroll 1961 and Sotelo 1973).

In the majority of states under consideration here, contemporary rural structures are dominated by small-scale farming on a family basis (see Table 1, column 9). This applies to the African countries, parts of the Carribean States, several Asian cases (including the special conditions in the Maldive Islands where fishing predominates) and present-day Egypt. Two exceptions on the Latin American continent are post-revolutionary Mexico with its strongly cooperative forms of agriculture ("ejidos") and Costa Rica with its considerable proportion of small-scale and middle-level immigrant farmers. As for the remaining Latin American countries (*e.g.* Colombia, the Dominican Republic and Venezuela), the characteristic latifundio-minifundio structures still persist. A number of other states (such as India, Malaysia, Mauritius and Trinidad/Tobago) exhibit mixed forms of large-scale land ownership and peasant farming with both traditional and modern elements (e.g. export-oriented plantations).

There can be no doubt that widespread small-scale farming in predominantly agrarian countries is an important factor in the emergence of democratic social and political structures. This recognition comes to light both in the "classical" middle class arguments of authors from Aristotle and de Toqueville to Dahl and in the concrete experiences of numerous contemporary 'First World" countries (for example the early United States, Canada, New Zealand, Switzerland, the Scandinavian countries etc.). Even in such cases, however, the commercialization of agriculture under contemporary conditions has eventually led to increased social differentiation. Conversely, it is safe to argue that feudal and "neo-feudal "forms of large-scale land ownership have retarded democratic forms of development (consider, for example the historical cases of Hungary or Romania—see Senghaas 1982—or the long history of unsuccessful attempts establish democratic regimes in Latin America). In view of the available data base it is difficult to quantify this factor more precisly. The existing Gini-coefficients for the distribution of agricultural land ownership (see Table 2, column 3) are incomplete and are based rather on inconsistent sources and categories.

Nevertheless, the great inequality which the Latin American states exhibit in this regard do become apparent.

The relationship between social differentiation and the formation of potential conflict groups in the non-agrarian sectors is even more difficult to assess. In "objective" terms one would first have to determine the proportions of different groups relative to the means of production and their resulting social dynamics over a period of time. This relationship should, in our opinion, not only concern with aspects of property rights but also include actual powers of decision-making (e.g. by high level management) and aspects of political control. In this way, a differentiated class model could be developed which would allow for an approximate assessment of potential social and economic conflict-groups on the basis of the criteria cited (cf., e.g., Berg-Schlosser 1979). Because of the "peripheral" position which the countries of the Third World occupy, the specific role and the share of foreign capital in these economies must also be taken into account. Moreover, in addition to these objective dimensions, the subjective perceptions and attitudes of these groups and their tendencies towards "closure" (cf., e.g., Parkin 1979) must be assessed. Except for a few case studies of a generally limited scope, however, there are no comparative let alone longitudinal data available on which such an analysis could be based.

The index of "class fractionalization" which indicates the proportional persons employed in the agricultural and non-agricultural sectors (cf., e.g., Lijphart 1977, pp. 71 ff.) provides a rough approximation in this regard. Because of the dominance of rural elements, the index shows rather low figures for most of the African and some of the Asian states in our sample. The Latin American countries as well as Botswana, Malaysia, Mauritius, Sri Lanka and Egypt reveal an almost equal balance between agricultural and non-agricultural employment while Singapore as a city state also scores very low (see Table 2, columns 4 and 5). A further indication of the formation of class structures is the degree of union organization. This varies with the proportion of non-agriculturally employed persons but is also dependent upon the more general "openness" of the political system and upon specific subjective factors conducive to workers' solidarity. Of the states under consideration here, union organization is the relatively high in Fiji, Venezuela, Sri Lanka, Mauritius and Barbados. It is comparatively low in Botswana, India and Kenya but also in Singapore when one considers the high level of industrialization there (see Table 2, column 6).

The share of foreign capital is extremely high in the economies of a number of countries under consideration here (see Table 2, column 10). This is particularly the case in Trinidad, Papua-New Guinea, Jamaica, Singapore, Venezuela, Costa

Rica, Malaysia, the Dominican Republic and Senegal. On the other hand, states like India, Sri Lanka and Egypt exhibit relatively low values. The width of distribution is therefore quite remarkable with respect to this variable also. Still, the mean of our sample is significantly higher than the mean for all Third World countries together. Foreign capital thus appears to possess a certain "affinity" towards more democratic forms of government, at least where these have proven to be somewhat more durable, although "neo-colonial" considerations most certainly play an important role here as well.

In accordance with Blau's model (1976,p.223), data on income distribution can be used as a "graduated" parameter of differentiation within the social structure. Here again, a "Gini index" is usually employed for the purpose of international comparison. Such indices, of course, are based purely on monetary a values and can at best provide only rough estimates with respect to subsistence forms of income. For countries with high levels of subsistence production in agriculture or with a considerable "shadow economy" in the "informal" sectors, an index of this kind proves rather unreliable. Moreover, the comparative international data which are available are not complete and the statistical base in the respective countries themselves (*e.g*, income statistics collected by taxation departments) is often highly dubious. This is true for a number of "First World" states and all the more so for the cases under consideration here. Among the latter, Sri Lanka, Barbados, Egypt and Costa Rica demonstrate a more eqalitarian distribution of income (see Table 2, columns 7 to 9). In contrast, the other Latin American states and the African countries exhibit strong income discrepancies. In Africa, there is a greater distortion resulting from the higher proportion of subsistence income that must be taken into account. For all Third World countries together, however, the deviation from the mean is not significant.

The actual formation of political conflict groups depends upon the concrete interaction between moments of horizontal and vertical social differentiation and the historical development of particular cleavages. (This has been demonstrated in an exemplary manner in the model developed for the Western European states by Lipset and Rokkan, 1977). Once again, mutually reinforcing levels of conflict prove the most intensive whereas a cross-cutting of conflict group may reduce social tensions. It is important to note, however, that even where conflicts are mainly expressed on the basis of horizontal differentiation, they only rarely constitute ethnic, religious or other communalistic antagonisms *per se* (such as those relating to the contents of different religious doctrines). On the contrary, in most crises they constitute struggle for the distribution of economic privileges and political power which only lead to processes of identification along communalistic lines on the level of subjective perceptions.

Because of the lack of appropriate data, the concrete cross-cutting of conflict groups in the countries of our sample cannot be quantified more precisely (*e.g.*, in the manner demonstrated by Rae and Taylor, 1970). As we have seen, most states under consideration here are pluralistic in a horizontal sense because of their artificial creation by the colonial powers. Nowadays they all exhibit a considerable measure of vertical conflict-group formation as well. An important indication of the interaction between these two dimensions is their representation within the existing party systems. In the great majority of states (17 out of 22), a dominance of class-based parties can be observed. In twelve of them, however, one finds a combination of class based parties and parties organized along religious, ethnic or regional lines (see Table 4, column 3). In four cases (Fiji, Kenya, Malaysia and Sri Lanka) the articulation of the horizontal conflict dimension appears to be dominant. This most likely applies potentially to the no-party state of the Maldives as well.

(*d*) *Socio-economic indicators*

As pointed out above, the majority of contemporary studies in "empirical democratic theory" is based upon socio-economic indicators. The available data enable us to test some of the major hypotheses of this approach for the 1960 to 1980 period (see Table 3). If we look at the four main variables of Lipset's (1960) study wealth, urbanization, literacy and mass communications). the considerable width of distribution, among the cases in our sample is striking. Four states (Gambia, India, the Maldives and Sri Lanka) belong to the "low-income countries" of World Bank statistics. In nine others (among them the remaining African states, Egypt and Papua-New Guinea in particular) "middle income" levels (up to US, 1600) prevail. The rest (in particular the majority of Latin American cases, Malaysia and Singapore) rank above this figure. The levels of industrialization (with very low values for Papua-New Guinea, Senegal, Kenya, India and Sri Lanka reveal a similar picture. The rates of urbanization are relatively low in these countries as well, whereas the Latin American states achieve high scores. Levels of literacy show a similarly wide distribution: they are very low for countries like Gambia, Senegal, Papua-New Guinea India and Botswana, medium in Egypt and kenya and high in the majority of Latin American states, Malaysia. Singapore and Sri Lanka. The scores relating to the distribution of the means of mass communication vary from very low for the Maldives, Kenya, Sri Lanka, India, Papua-New Guinea, Senegal and the Dominican Republic to high in the majority of Latin American states, Malaysia, Mauritius and Singapore. (The distribution of radio raceivers was selected as the most relevant indicator in this regard for Third World states). Standard deviations are all very high and there is a consider able intersection of these distribution patterns with those for other Third World system types and even for parts of the "Second" and "First" Worlds. Intercorrelations between these "modernization" variables range between .48 and .82 and are all statistically significant ($p<.01$). On the average, these figures are some what higher than those for the Third World as a whole (where they vary between .45 and .73) but are considerably lower than those for "First World" countries.

In terms of Deutsch's (1961) "social mobilization" hypothesis, the rates of change for these indicators reveal a similar picture.

High average rates of economic growth in countries linke Singapore, Malaysia, Botswana and Barbados contrast with patterns of stagnation and even a certain decline in Jamaica, Senegal and the Bahamas. Industrialization has increased considerably in Egypt and Singapore, but only very little in Colombia and India, and has stagnated in Jamaica and Sri Lanka. Colombia, the Dominican Republic, Mexico, venezuela and Papua show strong increases in their urban populations whereas in Senegal, Malaysia and India these remained relatively low. Literacy rates were greatly improved in Kenya, Mauritius and Singapore; in Senegal and Papua-New Guinea they remained almost stagnant on a fairly low level whereas in Barbados, and Venezuela they reached relatively high scroes. The distribution of radio receivers increased most rapidly in Barbados, Jamaica, Mexico and Trinidad/Tobago while in the Dominican Republic, Senegal and Sri Lanka there was very little change. Standard deviations for all these rates are rather high. Some of the intercorrelations are even negative and they are all non-significant. This also applies to the Third World as a whole and is thus in clear contradiction to Deutsch's hypothesis.

The "Physical Quality of Life Index" (PQLI)—an aggregate measure of life expectancy, infant mortality and literacy rates (see Morris 1979)—exhibits a rather wide range as well. The figures for countries like Senegal, Papua-New Guinea and India are very low but fairly high for most of the Latin America states, Sri Lanka and Singapore. The respective annual "Disparity Reduction Rates" (DRR) are equally uneven. Relative improvements have been the lowest in Trinidad and Tobago, the Dominican Republic and Egypt and the highest in Singapore, Jamaica and Costa Rica. Nonetheless, the mean PQLI is significantly higher for the systems under our consideration than for other system types or for the Third World as a whole (see Berg-Schlosser 1984a). If all the cases considered here are lumped together into a single category of "near-polyarchies" and are contrasted on a dichotomous basis with all other Third World systems, no statistically relevant figures (*i.e.* of at least $p < .05$) will emerge for either levels or for the rates of change in the indicators for wealth, industrialization, urbanization and mass communications. Only literacy has relatively low positive correlations for its level (r=.26, p .01) and rate of change (r=.18, p .05). All in all, therefore, the hypothesis put forward by "modernization theorists" concerning the relationship between the above mentioned indicators and the existence of stable democratic systems cannot be confirmed for the cases and the period considered here.

3. *Further procedures*

In order to assess the impact of different independent variables a series of stepwise multiple regressions was conducted. For this purpose, all the cases selected were once again lumped together and contrasted to all other Third World states as a dichotomized dependent variable. As it turned out, the absolute levels of Lipset's most important socio-economic indicators for the year 1980 "explain" only a small part of the variance: R^2=.166 (see Table 5a). Their rates of change for this period contribute even less: R^2=.152. The different signs for "Simple R" indicate that not all of these factors work in the same direction (see Table 5b).

The impact of different variables relating to the social structure produced a similarly heterogeneous picture (see Table 5 c). The Gini indices for the distribution of income and the pattern of land ownership and the indicators for penetration by multinational corporations and class fractionalization demonstrate weak negative correlations. On the other hand, there are weak positive correlations for factors like ethnolinguistic fractionalization, religious fractionalization and union organization. However, the total explained variance (R^2=.134) is again rather low. It must also be taken into account that the statistical bases for many of these variables are particulary unsatisfactory and that for many cases there is a large number of missing data. All in all, therefore, these findings prove to be of a basically negative nature.

In order to test the joint impact of different historical-cultural and social-structural factors, a series of analyses of variance were then conducted. Since the level of measurement for must variables of this kind is only of a nominal nature, multiple classification analyses were employed. In different combinations, it was attempted to assess the respective independent influence of the variables discussed above. It turned, out that of all the variables listed in Tables 1-3, region, former colonial power, agrarian structure and MNC-penetration were the most important (see values of beta in Table 6. Other factors such as dominant religion, religious and ethnic fractionalization, class fractionalization and the socio-economic variables previously discussed contributed relatively little over and above the observed variance (values of beta of .10 and below). Specific influences of political culture thus play a clearly important role as demonstrated by factors such as "region" and "former colonial power." In particular, the democratizing" effect of the British colonial heritage and certain positive influences in Asia and Latin America (most of all among the Carribean states) can be demonstrated in this way (see the signs of the deviations in Table 6).

A further factor, at least for those countries where the majority of the population is still employed in agriculture, is the agrarian structure. Here, traditional communal and other small-scale forms of farming apparently offer more favourable social conditions for the emergence of democratic political structures than large-scale latifundios or plantations. Moreover —and this may be somewhat surprising at first sight—a high level of MNC-penetration also works in a positive direction. Even though in other contexts—for example as far the degree of autonomy and self-determination of a country is concerned—this penetration may be viewed negatively, it does contribute to the maintenance of tendencially democratic structures possibly by means of certain "demonstration effects" resulting from close links with Western states. (The fact that, in a number of cases, multi-national corporations have closely cooperated with repressive regimes as long as their economic interests were safeguarded does not contradict this statement). In spite of the considerable higher level of variance which can be explained in this way (see values of multiple R and R^2), the heterogeneity of the cases considered remains remarkable.

A further "cluster analysis," led to the identification of certain sub-types. One cluster which can be termed "early democratic" comprises states with a low to medium level of socio-economic development, tendencially eqalitarian social traditions and a predominance of small-scale farming. Most of these countries had previously been under British colonial rule. Gambia, the Maldives, Papua-New Guinea and Senegal are examples of states belonging to this category. Cases exhibiting stronger elements of communalistic fractionalization such as Botswana, Fiji, Kenya or Malaysia reveal more consociational political structures. India with her very large population and federal structures is a further variant of this sub-type.

A second major cluster consists of states with relatively small populations, a high level of socio-economic development, traditions of British colonial rule and, in part, varying forms of plantation and other large-scale agriculture. This cluster may be termed "dependent democratic." Examples of this sub-type are Carribean states like the Bahamas, Barbados, Jamaica and Trinidad and Tobago as well as Mauritius, Singapore and Sri Lanka.

A third and last cluster which can be called "late democratic" encompasses countries of a generally larger size and with a high level of socio-economic development. These countries were subject to Spanish colonial traditions and exhibit an agrarian structure polarized into latifundios and minifundios. Only relatively recently have they developed more durable democratic structures. States like Colombia, the Dominican Republic and Venezuela are cases in point. Post-revolutionary Mexico with her "semi-competitive" structures constitutes a variant of this category. The renewed attempts in countries like Argentina, Brazil, Peru or Uruguay, and possibly even the Philippines may also, finally, follow this path (cf., *e.g.*, Mols 1985, Berg-Schlosser 1986a).

II: Conclusions

Despite its restriction to macro-quantitative aspects of the complex topic under examination, the preceding analysis has demonstrated the heterogeneity of democratic political systems in Third World countries and elaborated upon their broader social and economic conditions. Forms of democratization can be found in states of all sizes and in all regions, states with every type of colonial background possessing a large variety of socio-cultural traditions and exhibiting very different levels of socio-economic development. Overly simplistic "modernization" theories merely explain a fraction of this variance. One major result of this study is thus of a predominantly negative character inasmuch as it concerns the relevance of approaches of this kind.

Nonetheless, certain "positive" conclusions can also be drawn, albeit of a tentative nature. Rustow's (1970) "genetic" approach with respect to different phases in the emergence of democratic systems and their respective background conditions appears to be basically in line with the arguments advanced in this study. Relatively eqalitarian and decentralized social structures in the pre-colonial period were found to be favourable to the development of democratic systems in a number of states. Similarly, in countries with relatively low levels of socio-economic development, the dominance of commercial or small-scale forms of farming proved to be an important factor in this respect. "Habituation" to modern democratic procedures is a further important element which was found to be especially determining in the former British colonies. A high levels of penetration by Western multinational corporations appeared to have a similar effect (although this must be viewed as "neo-colonial" under other circumstances). All of these factors tended to be more effective in small-scale countries with relatively homogeneous social structures whereas federal structures were seen to provide the best basis for democracy in larger states. In confirmation of Lijphart's contention, consociational models of democracy appeared superior to the "Westminster" type in countries where "communalistic" conflicts tend to prevail. All in all, it was possible to specify more closely some of the conditions of democratic development broadly conceived by Dahl although others had to be substantially modified.

A side from these general factors and considerations, it was also possible to demonstrate the existence of certain characteristic clusters of democratic sub-types and to sketch their specific "paths" of development. The "early democratic" cluster represents the successful combination of eqalitarian pre-colonial conditions, the predominance of small-scale farming in its various forms and—in most cases—the influence of British political culture. A number of parallels can be drawn between this sub-type and other states (*e.g.*, Switzerland, the United States and the Scandinavian countries) which became democratic during periods of low social-economic development. A second sub-type, the "dependent democratic" cluster, consists of societies with essentially hierarchical traditions, a higher level of present-day socio-economic development and democratic political structures which were originally established under (British) colonial rule and subsequently maintained. Such countries are generally of smaller size, tend to be ethnically homogeneous and possess political systems of the "Westminster' type.

The "late democratic" cluster is basically a Latin American sub-type so far and deviates substantially from the above pattern. In this case, there exist neither eqalitarian pre-colonial traditions nor a phase of habituation to externally imposed democratic institutions. On the contrary, the specific agrarian structures and forms of political dominance which emerged during the period of Spanish colonial rule must be considered as particularly inimical to democratic forms of development. Improved prospects for the emergence of potentially durable forms of democratic government seem only to have arisen: (a) in the wake of successful revolutions which effectuated significant changes in the social structure (as in Mexico), or (b) in countries at a much higher stage of socio-economic development where the urban middle classes have become increasingly dominant.

As the Latin American experience demonstrates, stable democracies require a specific phase of habituation and "internalization" at the micro-level of participant political behaviour as well as the emergence of a generally democratic political culture. This, however, constitutes no easy process in view of continuing social tensions and the perseverance of diverse forms of international economic (for more skeptical assessments see also Huntington 1984, Jackson and Rosberg 1985) and political dependence. The above conclusions can, of course, only constitute fairly rough approximations and are necessarily of a preliminary nature. In order to test our main propositions in greater detail, both further comprehensive case studies with a more profound historical dimension, such as those presently being undertaken in the course of a large research project at Stanford University directed by S.M. Linsetand J. Lin and additional comparative analyses with considerably improved data bases such a those prepared by Tatu Vanhanen (1984), for example, will be required.

Aside from these purely empirical questions, however, the realization of adapted forms of democracy in Third World countries still presents a prime normative challenge. As has been shown above, there is a much larger variety of factors at work here than implied by "modernization theories" many of which have been conceived in a thoroughly deterministic manner. Moreover, a lesser degree of socio-economic determination also provides the actors responsible with greater room to maneouver. The failure of democracy in Third World countries need no longer constitute a "self-fulfilling prophecy" for political scientists nor most it provide a cheap justification for authoritarian rulers. Although the roads to the realization of more humane, just and participatory forms of government are by no means easy and although different parts of the world may require different "paths"—these roads remain not only the concern of political science but, even more important, of the populations in the states concerned.

TABLE 1

Country	*Region*	*Pre-colon. social struct.*	*Former colon. power*	*Colonial "mise en valeur"*	*Year of indepen-dence*	*Pol. syst. since*	*Dominant religion*	*Ethnic composition*	*Dominant agrarian structure*
1	*2*	*3*	*4*	*5*	*6*	*7*	*8*	*9*	*10*
Bahamas	Latin Amer.	—	UK	trade	1973	1964	Prot.	80% negr. 10% Mul. 10% white	small farms
Barbados	Latin Amer.	—	UK	plant	1966	1966	Prot.	90% negr. 6% Mul. 4% white	plantations
Botswana	Africa	hierarch.	UK	labor	1966	1966	trad.	80% Botsw. 12% Bakal.	small farms
Colombia	Latin Amer.	hierarch.	Spain	plant.	1810	1968	Cath.	66% Mest. 20% white 7% Indios	latif./ minif.
Costa Rica	Latin Amer.	—	Spain	plant.	1821	1949	Cath.	80% white 15% Mest. 4% negr.	small and middle farms

(*Contd.*)

1	2	3	4	5	6	7	8	9	10
Domin. Rep.	Latin Amer.	—	Spain	trade	1844	1966	Cath.	60% Mul. 28% white 11% negr.	latif./ minif.
Egypt	Middle East	"hydraul"	UK	raw materials	1922	1970	Islam	93% Arab	small farms
Fiji	Asia	hierarch.	UK	raw materials	1970	1970	Christian	50% Indian 44% Fijians	small farms
Gambia	Africa	hierarch.	UK	trade	1965	1965	Islam	41% Mandingo 14% Fulani 13% Wolof	small farms
India	Asia	hierarch.	UK	raw materials	1947	1947	Hindu	72% Northern 25% Southern	large farms/ small farms
Jamaica	Latin Amer.	—	UK	plant.	1962	1962	Prot.	77% negr. 18% Mul.	large farms
Kenya	Africa	eqal.	UK	settlers	1963	1963	mixed Christians	20% Kikuyu 14% Luo 13% Luyia	small farms

Maldives	Asia	hierarch.	UK	trade	1965	1965	Islam	mixed Sinhalese	fishermen
Malaysia	Asia	hierarch.	UK	plant	1957	1957	Islam/ Hindu/ Buddhist	47% Malayis. 33% Chinese 9% Indian	plantations/ small farms
Mauritius	Africa	—	UK	plant	1968	1968	Hindu/ Christian	70% Indo-Mauritian/ 26% Creoles	plantations/ small farms
Mexico	Latin Amer.	hierarch.	Spain	mining	1810	1917	Cath.	97% Mest. 2% Indios 1%	Co-operati-ves/small farms
Papua/N.G.	Asia	eqal.	UK	raw materials	1975	1964	Prot.	99% Melanes.	small farms
Senegal	Africa	hierarch.	France	raw materials	1960	1960	Islam	36% Wolof 16% Serer 17% Fulani	small farms
Singapore	Asia	—	UK	trade	1965	1965	Buddhist/ Islam	76% Chinese 15% Malays. 7% Indian	—

(*Contd.*)

1	2	3	4	5	6	7	8	9	10
Sri Lanka	Asia	hierarch.	UK	raw materials	1948	1948	Buddhist	72% Sinhal. 20% Tamil	small farms
Trinidad/ Tobago	Latin Amer.	—	UK	trade	1962	1962	mixed Christian	43% negr. 41% Indian	small farms
Venezuela	Latin Amer.	hierarch.	Spain	plant.	1811	1961	Cath.	67% Mest./ Mul. 21% white 10% negr.	latif./ minif.

Sources: Banks and Overstreet 1983, Draguhn 1980, Hofmeier 1984, Kurian 1982, Nohlen and Nuscheler 1982 ff. vol. 2-8; Steinbach 1979, Waldmann 1982.

TABLE 2

Social Structural Indicators

Country	*Ethnic fract. ca. '60*	*Relig, fract. '75*	*Giniland ca. '60-'70*	*Class.— fract. '60*	*Class.— fract. '77*	*Union Organiz. (%) '75*	*Gini-income ca. '70*	*Income top 5%*	*Income lowest 40%*	*MNC penetration ca '73*
1	*2*	*3*	*4*	*5*	*6*	*7*	*8*	*9*	*10*	*11*
Bahamas		0.42				25	46.7	20.7	12.2	
Barbados	0.22	0.25		0.38		32	36.9	19.8	18.6	
Botswana	0.51	0.62	59.8	0.15		2	57.4	28.1	7.6	
Colombia	0.06	0.06	86.4	0.5	0.43	13	56.2	33.7	10.0	52
Costa Rica	0.07	0.17	80.3	0.5	0.42	12	44.5	23.0	12.0	152
Domin. Rep.	0.04	0.06	80.3	0.44	0.49	12	49.3	26.3	12.4	145
Egypt	0.04	0.20	67.4	0.49	0.50	20	43.4	19.2	14.1	36
Fiji		0.65		0.16		50	42.3	19.0	14.8	

(*Contd.*)

1	*2*	*3*	*4*	*5*	*6*	*7*	*8*	*9*	*10*	*11*
Gambia	0.73	0.26		0.25		25				
India	0.89	0.36	64.0	0.38	0.39	3	47.8	25.0	17.2	7
Jamaica	0.05	0.43	78.4	0.48	0.36	25	57.7	30.2	8.2	167
Kenya	0.83	0.78	69.2	0.24	0.33	8	63.7	46.2	9.5	53
Maldives	0.18	0.0								
Malaysia	0.72	0.67	3.47	0.47	0.49	15	51.8	28.3	10.6	149
Mauritius	0.58	0.66		0.48		35				
Mexico	0.30	0.08	73.2	0.49	0.45	20	58.3	37.8	10.3	49
Papua/N.G.	0.42	0.50		0.20	0.27					169
Senegal	0.72	0.17		0.27	0.35		58.8	36.8	9.4	140
Singapore	0.42	0.60		0.15	0.04					160
Sri Lanka	0.47	0.51		0.49	0.50	43	35.3	18.6	19.2	31
Trinidad/Tob.	0.56	0.71	69.1	0.34	0.23	30				170
Venezuela	0.11	0.10	93.2	0.45	0.33	45	54.5	27.2	10.3	156

mean	0.39	0.38	69.8	0.36	0.36	20.47	50.8	27.5	12.3	107.1
standard dev.	0.28	0.25	15.1	0.14	0.13	13.06	8.3	7.9	3.5	46.6
For comparison:										
mean of total Third World	0.44	0.41	64.2		0.37	19.1	48.6	27.0	13.4	72.5
standard dev.	0.30	0.21	18.4		0.12	18.6	9.7	8.2	4.3	55.1

Sources: Taylor and Jodice 1983; Bornschier and Heintz 1979.

TABLE 3

Socio-economic indicators 1960—80

Country	*Pop. '80 (mill.)*	*Pop. growth 60-80*	*GNP/cap. '80 (U.S.$)*	*GNP/c. growth 60-80*	*Ind. '80 (% labour force)*	*Rate of Industr. 60-80*	*Urb. '80 (%)*	*Rate of Urbn. 60-80*	*Lit. '80 (%)*	*Rate of lit 60-80*	*Radios '79 (per 1000 pop.)*	*Rate of change radios 60-79*	*PQLI '80*	*DRR 60-80*
1	2	3	4	5	6	7	8	9	10	11	12	13	14	15
Bahamas	0.2	3.4	3.790	—0.8					93	0.20	442			
Barbados	0.2	0.8	3.040	4.5					98	0.15	524	19.68		
Botswana	0.8	1.7	910	9.2					35	0.75	82	4.00		
Colombia	26.70	2.7	1.180	3.0	21	0.10	70	1.10	81	0.80	114	—1.32	77	2.8
Costa Rica	2.2	2.4	1.730	3.2	23	0.20	43	0.30	90	0.30	82	0.84	89	3.5
Domin. Rep.	5.4	3.0	1.160	3.4	18	0.30	51	1.05	67	0.10	41	0.37	69	0.9
Egypt	39.8	2.1	580	3.4	30	0.90	45	0.35	44	0.70	132	3.89	54	0.9
Fiji	0.6	2.0	1.850	3.3					75		485			

Gambia	0.6	2.6	250	1.7					15	0.25	109	5.42		
India	673.2	2.2	240	1.4	13	0.10	22	0.20	35	0.35			45	1.4
Jamaica	2.2	1.5	1.040	0.6	25	0.00	41	0.35	90	0.25	332	12.84	90	3.6
Kenya	15.9	3.5	420	2.7	10	0.25	14	0.35	47	1.20	35	1.37	55	1.8
Maldives	0.2	3.8	260	1.3					82		28			
Malaysia	13.9	2.8	1.620	4.3	16	0.20	29	0.20	60	0.85	150	5.95	73	2.3
Mauritius	0.9	1.5	1.060	2.3					85	1.25	196	7.11		
Mexico	69.8	3.6	2.090	2.6	26	0.30	67	0.80	83	0.90	288	10.16	79	2.6
Papua/N.G.	3.0	2.2	780	2.8	8	0.20	18	0.75	32	0.15	52		45	1.2
Senegal	5.7	2.6	450	—0.3	10	0.25	25	0.10	10	0.10	54	0.37	25	1.0
Singapore	2.4	1.5	4.430	7.5	39	0.80	100	0.00	83	1.15	179	4.84	89	4.3
Sri Lanka	14.7	1.6	270	2.4	14	0.00	27	0.45	85	0.50	47	0.58	82	2.0
Trinidad/Tob.	1.2	1.6	4.370	3.0	39	0.25	21	—0.05	95	0.75	263	9.32	92	0.5
Venezuela	14.9	3.0	3.630	2.6	27	0.25	83	0.80	82	0.10			82	2.0

(Contd.)

1	2	3	4	5	6	7	8	9	10	11	12	13	14	15
mean			1532.73	3.04	20.19	0.26	41.75	0.45	65.64	0.55	158.65	5.08	67.78	2.32
standard dev.			1403.03	2.31	10.48	0.25	26.24	0.35	27.32	0.39	143.20	5.48	19.81	1.25
For comparison:														
Monarchies/Olig.			4116	3.2	15.6	0.20	38.4	0.70	47.7	0.80	151.5	3.80	54.50	1.80
Soz./Comm.Systems			566	2.3	18.2	0.30	36.3	0.60	59.4	1.10	109.2	4.00	58.10	2.40
Mil./praet. Systems			1005	2.1	15.2	0.20	34.4	0.60	48.2	0.80	114.2	4.30	50.10	1.60
Total Third World			1982+	2.6^0	16.70	0.20^0	37.3^0	0.600	53.6$^+$	0.80^0	139.9^0	4.40^0	55.60$^+$	1.90

Levels of significance: 0=not significant, +=$p<0.05$
Sources: Taylor and Jodice 1983; World Bank 1983.

TABLE 4

System characteristics

	Party System			Dominant articulated cleavages	Head of executive		Separation of powers vertical horizontal				Formation of government		
	One Party with competetive elemets	*restricted multi-party*	*open multi-party*		*President*	*Prime Minister*	*full*	*limited with independent judiciary*	*federal*	*centralised*	*competitive*	*consociational*	*Electrical participation (%, latest available figures)*
1	*2*	*3*	*4*	*5*	*6*	*7*	*8*	*9*	*10*	*11*	*12*	*13*	*14*
Bahamas			X	class (ethn.)		X		X		X	X		79
Barbados			X	class		X		X		X	X		
Botswana			X	class (ethn.)	X		X			X		X (hegem.)	
Colombia		X		class (rel.)		X	X		X		X	(X) (until/74)	36
Costa Rica			X	class	X		X			X	X		70

(*Contd.*)

1	*2*	*3*	*4*	*5*	*6*	*7*	*8*	*9*	*10*	*11*	*12*	*13*	*14*
Dominic. Rep.		X		class	X		X			X	X	X (in parl.)	63
Egypt		X		class (rel.)	X			X		X		X (hegem.)	21
Gambia			X	class (ethn.)	X			X		X	X		70
India			X	class (rel.)		X		X	X		X		67
Jamaica			X	class		X		X		X	X		85
Kenya	X			class (ethn.)	X			X		X		X	60
Maldives	X			regional	X			X		X		X	
Malaysia			X	class (ethn.)	X			X	X			X	41
Mauritius			X	class (ethn.)		X		X		X	X		
Mexico		X		class	X		X		X			X (hegem.)	63
Papua/N.G.			X	ethn./rel.,cl.		X		X		X	X		
Senegal			X	ethn./rel., gl.	X		X			X	X		65
Singapore		X		class (ethn.)		X		X		X		X (hegem.)	67
Sri Lanka			X	class (ethn.)	X		X			X	X		71
Trinidad/Tob.			X	class (ethn.)		X		X		X	C		64
Venezuela			X	class (rel.)	X		X		X		X		80

Source: see Table 1 and Taylor and Jodice 1983.

TABLE 5

Multiple Regressions

(a) Socio-economic indicators *Levels 1980*

Independent variable	*Simple*	*Multiple R*	R^2
Industrialization	0.312	0.312	0.097
Literacy	0.311	0.358	0.128
Urbanization	0.162	0.386	0.149
Radios 1000 pop.	0.137	0.401	0.161
GNP/cap.	0.015	0.407	0.166

(b) Socio-economic indicators *Rates of change 1960-1980*

Independent Variable	*Simple R*	*Multiple R*	R^2
Rate of urbanization	0.196	0.196	0.039
Rate of GNP cap. growth	—0.173	0.321	0.103
Rate of literacy increase	0.164	0.376	0.142
Rate of industrialization	—0.157	0.386	0.149
Rate of radio increase	—0.069	0.390	0.152

(c) Quantitative social structural variables *ca. 1970—75*

Independent variable	*Simple R*	*Multiple R*	R^2
Ethno-linguist. fractionalization	0.204	0.204	0.042
Gini income	—0.147	0.254	0.065
Religious fractionalization	0.001	0.284	0.080
Union organization (per cent labor force)	0.047	0.320	0.102
Gini-land	—0.130	0.352	0.124
MNC-penetration	—0.164	0.364	0.133
Class fractionalization	—0.007	0.365	0.134

Sources: Taylor and Jodice 1983, World Bank 1983, Bornschier and Heintz 1979.

TABLE 6

Multiple Classification Analysis

Independent variables	*Adjusted for independents deviations*	*beta*	*N*
Region:			
Africa	−1.32		28
Asia	+0.39		15
Latin America	+2.04		21
Middle East	−0.97	0.40	12
Former colonial power:			
United Kingdom	+1.48		20
France	−0.65		21
Spain	+0.35		17
other/no	−1.22	0.30	18
Dominant agrarian structure:			
Traditional peasant or small farms	+0.36		50
Feudal or large farms	+0.83		5
Latifundios or plantations	−1.47		15
State or collective farms	−0.04	0.29	6
MNC-penetration:			
Low	−0.08		39
Medium	−1.91		17
High	+1.78	0.37	20

Multiple R: 0.630
R^2 : 0.397

REFERENCES

Almond, G.A. and J.S. Coleman (eds.) (1960), The Politics of the Developing Areas, Princeton: Princeton University Press.

and S. Verba (1963), The Civic Culture, Princeton: Princeton University Press.

(eds.) (1980 , The Civic Culture Revisited, Boston: Little, Brown.

Banks, A.S. and R.B. Textor (1963), A cross-Polity Survey, Cambridge/ Mass.: M.I.T. Press.

(1972), "Correlates of Democratic Performance," Comparative Politics, January, pp. 217-230.

and W. Overstreet (1983), Political Handbook of the World: 1982-1983, New York: Mc Graw-Hill.

Barkan, J.D. and Okumu (eds.) (1979), Politics and Public Policy in Kenya and Tanzania, New York: Praeger.

Berg-Schlosser, D. (1979), "Soziale Differenzierung and Klassenbildung in Kenia—Entwicklungen und Perspektiven," Politische Vierteljahresschrift, vol. 20, no. 4, pp. 313-329.

(1982), "Modes and meaning of political participation in Kenya," Comparative Politics, July pp. 397-415.

(1984a), "African Political Systems—Typology and Performance," Comparative Political Studies, vol. 17, no. 1, pp. 121-151.

(1984b), "Third World Political Systems: Classification and Evaluation," paper presented at the annual meeting of the American Political Science Association. Washington/D.C.

(1985), "Zu den Bedingungen von Demokratie in der Dritten Welt, in: Nuscheler F. (ed.) Dritte Welt Forschung, Politische Vierteljahresschrift, Sonderheft 16, pp. 233.266.

(1986a), "Vormarsch der Demokratie in der Dritten Welt?" in: Jahrbuch Dritte Welt 1986, Munich: Beck.

(1986b), "Politische Kulturen," in Nohlen, D. and P. Waldmann (eds.), Pipers Wortherbuch zur Politik, vol. 6, Dritte Welt, Munich: Piper.

Blau, P.M. (1976), "Parameters of Social Structure," in: idem (ed.) Approaches to the Study of Social Structure, London: Open Books, pp. 220-253.

Bollen, K.A. (1980), "Issues in the Comparative Measurement of Political Democracy," American Sociological Review, June, pp. 370-390.

Bornschier, V. and P. Heintz (1979), Compendium of Data for World-System Analysis, Zurich: Soziologisches Institut.

Carroll, T.F. (1961), "The Land Reform Issue in Latin America," in: A.O. Hirschmann (ed.), Latin American Issues, New York: The Twentieth Century Fund, pp. 161-201.

Coquery—Vidrovitch, C. (1976), "The political economy of the African peasantry and modes of production," in: P.C.W. Gutkind and I. Wallerstein (eds.). The Political Economy of Contemporary Africa, beverly Hills: Sage, pp. 90-111.

Coulter, P. (1975), Social Mobilization and Liberal Democracy, Lexington/Mass.: Lexington Books.

Cutright, P. (1963), "National Political Development: Measurement and Analysis," American Sociological Review, April, pp. 253-264.

Dahl, R.A. (1971), Polyarchy—Participation and Opposition, New Haven: Yale University Press.

and E.R. Tufte (1973), Size and Democracy, Stanford: Stanford University Press.

Deutsch, K.W. (1961), "Social Mobilization and Political Development," American Political Science Review, vol. 60, no. 3, pp. 493-514.

Draguhn, W. *et. al.*, (1980), Politisches Lexikon Asien und Sudpazifik, Munchen: Beck.

Eckstein, H. (ed.) (1966), "A Theory of Stable Democracy" in: idem, Division and Cohesion in Democracy—A study of Norway, Princeton: Princeton University Press, Appendix B. pp. 225-288.

Flanigan, W. and E. Fogelman (1971a), "Patterns of political development and democratization: a quantitative analysis," in: J.V.

Gillespie and B.A. Nesvold (eds.). Macro-Quantitative Analysis-Conflict, Development and Democratization, Beverly Hills: Sage, pp. 441-473.

(1971b), "Patterns of Democratic Development: An Historical Comparative Analysis," in: Gillespie and Nesvold, *op. cit.*, pp. 475-497.

Gastil, R.D. (1978 ff.) Freedom in the World, New York: Freedom House.

Hermet, G. *et. al.*, (ed.) (1978), Elections without Choice, London: Macmillan.

Hofmeier, R. *et. al.*, (ed.), (1984), Politisches Lexikon Afrika, Munchen: Beck.

Huntington, S.P. (1966), "The Political Modernization of Traditional Monarchies," Deadalus, vol. 95, no. 3, pp. 763 ff.

and J.I Dominguez (1975), "Political Development" in: F.I. Greenstein and N.W. Polsby (eds.) Handbook of Political Science. vol. 3, Reading Pass.: Addison-Wesley, pp. 1-114.

(1984), "Will more countries become democratic?," Political Science Quarterly, vol. 93, pp. 193-218.

Jackson, R.H. and Rosberg, C.G. (1985), "Democracy in Tropical Africa," Journal of International Affairs, pp. 293-305.

Kurian, G.T. (1982), Encyclopaedia of the Third World, London: Mansell.

Lenski, G. (1966), Power and Privilege—A Theory of social Stratification, New York: Mc Graw-Hill.

Lerner, Daniel (1958), The Passing of Traditional Society, New York, The Free Press.

Lijphart, A. (1977), Democracy in Plural Societies, New Haven: Yale University Press.

(1984), Democracies, New Haven: Yale University Press.

Linz, Juan, J. (1975), "Totalitarian and Authoritarian Regimes," in: Greenstein and Polsby, *op. cit.* pp. 175-411.

and A. Stepan (eds.) (1978), The Breakdown of Democratic Regimes, Baltimore: Johns Hopkins Press.

Lipset, S.M. (1960), Political Man—The Social Bases of Politics, New York: Doubleday.

(1981), Political Man, expanded edition, Baltimore: Johns Hopkins Press.

and S. Rokkan (eds.) (1967), Party Systems and Voter Alignments, New York: The Free Press.

May, J.D. (1973), On the Conditions and Measures of Democracy, Morristown: General Learning Press.

Mc Rae, K. (ed.) (1974), Consociational Democracy, Toronto: McClelland and Stewart.

Melson, R. and H. Wolpe (1970), "Modernization and the Politics of Communalism—A Theoretical Prespective," American Political Science Review, vol. 64, pp. 1112-1130.

Middleton, J. and D. Tait (1958), Tribes without Rulers, London: Routledge and Kegan Paul.

Migdal, J.S. (1983), "Studying the Politics of Development and Change: The State of the Art," in: A.W. Finifter (ed.) Political Science—The State of the Discipline, Washington/D.C.: American Political Science Association.

Milne, R.S. (1981), Politics in Ethnically Bipolar States, Vancouver: University of British Columbia Press.

Mols, M. (1985), Demokratie in Lateinamerika, Stuttgart: Kohlhammer.

Moore, B. (1966), Social Origins of Dictatorship and Democracy, Boston: Beacon Press.

Morris, M.E. (1979), "Measuring the Condition of the World's Poor," New York: Pergamon.

Nohlen, D. and F. Nuscheler (eds.) (1982ff) Handbuch der Dritten Welt, 8 vols., Hamburg: Hoffmann und Campe.

Nordlinger, E.A. (1972), Conflict Regulation in Divided Societies, Cambridge/Mass.: Center for International Affairs, Harvard University.

Packard, R.M. (1981), Chiefship and Cosmology—An Historical Study of Political Competition, Bloomington: Indiana University Press.

Paden, J. (1973), Religion and Political Culture in Kano, Berkeley: University of California Press.

Padover, S.K. (ed.), (1965) The Forging of American Federalism, Selected Writings of James Madison, New York.

Parkin, F. (1979), Marxism and Class Theory, London: Tavistock.

Powell, G.B. (1981), "Party Systems and Political System Performance: Participation, Stability and Violence in Contemporary Democracies," American Political Science Review, vol. 75, pp. 861-879.

Pride, R.A. (1970), Origins of Democracy: A Cross-National Study of Mobilization, Party Systems and Democratic Stability, Beverly Hills; Sage.

Rae, D.W. and W. Taylor (1970), The Analysis of Political Cleavages, New Haven: Yale University Press.

Ragin, Charles C. (1981), "Comparative Sociology and the Comparative Method," International Journal of Comparative Sociology XXII, 1-2, 102-120.

Rouque, A. (1985), La Democratie, Paris: A.M. Metailie.

Rustow, D.A. (1967), A World of Nations: Problems of Political Modernization, Washington/D.C.: Brookings.

(1970), "Transitions to Democracy—Toward a Dynamic Model," Comparative Politics, vol. 2, pp. 337-363.

Senghaas, D. (1982), Von Europa lernen—Entwicklungsgeschichtliche Betrachtungen, Frankfurt: Suhrkamp.

Smith, A.K. (1969), "Socio—Economic Development and Political Democracy: A Causal Analysis," Midwest Journal of Political Science, vol. 13, pp. 95-125.

Sofri, G. (1979), Il modo di produzione asiatico, Torino: Giulio Einaudi.

Sotelo, I. (1973), Soziologie Lateinamerikas, Stuttgart: Kohlhammer.

Steinbach, U, *et al.* (eds.) (1979), Politisches Lexikon Nahost, Munchen: Beck.

Taylor, C.L. and D.A. Jodice (1983) (eds.), Handbook of Social and Political Indicators, third edition, 2 vols., New Haven: Yale University Press.

Tetzlaff, R. (1977), "Staat und Klasse in peripher-kapitalistischen Gesellschaftsformationen: Die Entwicklung des abhangigen Staatskapitalismus in Afrika," Verfassung und Recht in Ubersee, no. 1.

Vanhanen, Tatu (1984), The Emergence of Democracy, Helsinki: Societies Scientiarum Fennica.

Muldmann, P. (ed.) (1982), Politisches Lexikon Lateinamerika Munchen: Beck.

Wittfogel, K.A. (1957), Oriental Despotism, New Haven: Yale University Press.

World Bank (1979ff). World Development Report. Washington/D.C.

Ziemer, K. (1984), Demokratisierung in Westafrika? Paderborn: F. Schoeningh.

7

AUTHORITARIAN DEMOCRATIZATION OR GRANTED DEMOCRACY? FROM THE PAST TO THE PRESENT

GUY HERMET

> "*A bad despot, when his own personal indulgences have been provided for, may sometimes be willing to let the people alone; but a good deposit insists on doing them good, by making them do their own business in a better way than they themselves know of.*"
>
> —JOHN STUART MILL

The study of dictatorship and democracy: an historical perspective

Two prejudices of "old" political science hindered the study of the disturbing reality of authoritarian phenomena. Bernard Crick summarized the first one in saying that politics should be viewed as a "way of ruling in divided societies without undue violence": and that, on the basis of this postulate, political science could not be applied but "with great difficulty in non-political systems, and (did) not exist at all, as a free science, in anti-political regimes" (Crick: 1971, 141 and 163).

Thus, the cause of authoritarian systems as objects of analysis was lost from the start. Furthermore, the methodological and conceptual deficiencies caused by this way of viewing politics became a virtue, which disqualified right away the incomprehensible obstinacy of the researchers interested in authoritarianism. Hence the second prejudice. Authoritarianism remained for some an object of analysis. But this object could only be considered as the infra-political manifestation of an incapacity to govern, which was supposedly typical of the Third World underdeveloped societies (or those of the backward and meridional fringe of the Western World). Under these conditions, its study did not belong to the political scientist in the full sense of the word. It constituted the space voluntarily sacrificed to the subsidiary rank of area studies specialists. The analysis of authoritarian systems was illegitimate for two reasons: first because it seemed anti-political and unhealthy with regards to a—in fact idealized—concept of democratic power and of its pacific conquest; secondly, because scientifically infeasible or uninteresting, and for this reason, just good enough to delight the perverse connoisseurs of the unfathomable machinations of the oriental despots.

Then came Apter and Huntington, who reintegrated the study of exotic powers in a sub-heading of political sociology in the professional sense of the word. Then above all Juan Linz, who made the research on authoritarianism a part of the study of Western political systems (it being understood that dictatorships had never ceased to be one of "our" forms of government, even if they did escape the perceptive capacities of political scientists). Thanks to his pioneering contribution of 1964 (Linz: 1964), authoritarianism became again a concept even to the enthnocentric political science. Better still: the authoritarian situations become analyzable from the inside—no longer only salvageable in the typologies—thanks to the numerous methodological proposals that Linz enounced in his later works, starting with Francoist Spain, then Brazil after 1964 or Germany and Italy before 1945.

Reinserted into the range of regimes worthy of the attention of professional research, authoritarianism nevertheless continued to find itself confined to the minor grouping of the political breakdowns which took place in certain societies of central and meridional Europe or in Latin America (Linz: 1978). None, or almost none, dared acknowledge that the authoritarian experiences contributed slightly less than democratic experiences to the dynamic of political modernity in the Euro-American World. That authoritarianism represented not only one of the paths to this modernity, as underlined by Barrington Moore (1966), but that it had left a critical legacy, or even positive effects which, in the long term, transcended the organisation of power at a given moment. Barrington Moore only underlined the reality, the relative efficiency, even the normalcy of the authoritarian path to political modernity in the Western world, particularly in Germany. But even though he disputed the idealist or Marxist myopia which reduces Euro-American authoritarianism to an exceptional power of almost pathological nature, he did not break down the impenetrable barrier which was intended to separate it from the democratic highway of political development.

In fact, this barrier is nothing but a *cordon sanitaire* erected for intellectual and ideological reasons. Still today, it only preserves the conformism of the scholars who, for example, question what is normal and what is critical—that is a legacy of a non-democratic tradition—in the German political culture (Roberts: 1984). But the barrier does not exist in the facts. The influences from which arise the value systems and the attitudes of the West Germans are many and intercrossed, as are those which affect other peoples. Beyond this, two notes of greater importance should be suggested to those who consider the Western political dynamics. The first touches on the positive contributions that certain authoritarian regimes have brought to this dynamics, including in terms democratic progress or of the establishment of propitious conditions for it. More immediate, the second concerns the very realisation of the transition to democracy during the last few years. For at least a decade, the democratic "aberturas" carried out in Southern Europe and Latin America were more often the products of operations conceived of by leaders of authoritarian backgrounds, than the fruit of a conquest of liberty led by a democratic counterelite. Nowadays, democracy is more frequently granted than conquered.

Hence the purpose of this chapter, which consists in stressing a few paths for research on the role that contemporary authoritarianism plays in the construction of democracy. Franz Neumann noted, close to forty years ago, that "the relationship between democracy and dictatorship is not as simple as it is sometimes stated" (Neumann: 1957, 248). In so doing, he stressed the first dimension of a modernizing authoritarianism which for a long time has been "on the frontier of democracy" (Hermet: 1983). This, because it prepared the way to democracy by transforming its social context and by levelling certain old political barriers. Even if modern analysts don't think it necessary, a historical review of the para-democratic product of different dictatorial regimes of the last century serves as an illustration of this idea.

Way before Theodore Zeldin, Andre Siegfried (1913: 285) emphasized all that the French republican tradition owed to the semi-dictatorship exerted by Napoleon III from 1852 to 1870: first of all, an installed and practiced universal suffrage took root starting in this period. But Walter Bagehot caught even earlier the significance of the plebiscitary artifice, which permitted to transform the democratic "abertura" of this time in a set of attractive novelties which do not hurt" (Bagehot: 1964-1867, 203). The eminent English political essayist of Disraeli's period had understood right away a type of genius which mixed the authoritarian resource with the populist one. This invention muffled the inevitable eruption of the popular electorate by first domesticating it through the concession of "anxiously considered portions" of liberty, before returning it "its arbitrary power" after a decade of plebiscitarian apprenticeship. This when, in other countries, the parliamentary pre-democracies were still reduced to the polltaxes deterrence, or even to direct electoral fraud when they could not absorb by other means the establishment of universal suffrage.

But the truth is that Bagehot appreciated less the virtues of the other semi-imperial authoritarianism incarnated by Bismarck in Germany. For him, "Herr Von Bismarck, First Minister under the Prussian government, is becoming a public nuisance." In fact, the British essayist lacked only historical distance. Of course, there is no doubt that the architect of the German Empire could not play as well as Napoleon III with the resource offered by universal suffrage (in particular because of the religious splits which divide the electorate). Nevertheless, he used it as a not negligible instrument in the formation of a unified national identity. Better still, he compensated this partial electoral weakness by the invention of an other process of conservative integration of the masses: that of a welfare state which remained for a long time a specificity of Bismarckian authoritarianism, before being imitated by the North and West European democracies (Alder: 1976). For want of capacity to exercise the nascent social-democracy at the electoral level, the German Chancellor spirited away from the social-democrats the least disquieting fraction of their programme. In so doing, he determined the dominant reformist orientation of the German working class.

Reminders of this sort could be extended by the light of more recent--and often more discussed—examples of authoritarian induction of certain elements of political modernity in Western societies. Thus Brazil, where the populist authoritarianism incarnated from 1930 to 1954 Getulio Vargas, founded not only many democratic streams which persisted later on, but established also the bases of active citizenship and new expectations in the popular masses (until then enslaved by local potentates or misled into the ventures of milleniarisms without end). The same could be said about Mexico, where in spite of the hegemony exerted for decades by the clique of a pseudo-revolutionary and crypto-authoritarian dominant party, the monopolistic exercise of power brings with it a democratic pulse which mobilizes the whole society. Moreover, in spite of the hatred everybody feels for the Fascist and Nazi dictatorships, one has to admit that, even in these cases, authoritarianism removed some obstacles to the delayed democratization of Italy and Germany.

The fascist regime initiated the economic modernization of Italy. In so doing, it contributed to the shaking up of a society submitted to the domination of a traditional oligarchy which had reduced democracy to the rank of a political parody. More broadly, as Otto Bauer was amongst the first to underline (Bauer: 1967, 143-167), Fascism and Nazism channeled up the anti-oligarchic revolt of the middle classes frustrated from power. Specially in the case of Germany these dictatorships attached themselves in a systematic manner to destroy the power and social prestige of the old dominant groups represented by the aristocracy, the army, the upper level civil servants and the great industrial or financial bourgeoisie. By definitively crushing the status of these formerly hegemonic groups, they orchestrated, according to Vajda (1979: 9-13), a more meritocratic access to the spheres of greater responsibility. In other words as Ralf Dahrendorf said before Bauer, they started a process of socio-political modernization which was more founded on the "autonomous equallity of opportunity for all men" (Dahrendorf: 1962, 381). Whatever may be the horror caused by Nazism, this equalitarian and even levelling or "mediocratic" dimension (Hermet: 1983, 142) exists. In spite of it all, and without pardoning any of it, it represents a positive contribution to the ulterior democratic momentum of Germany. A momentum which Nazi paroxystic violence helped to unleash from the unchanging hierarchies which opposed until then the alignment of Germany to the political destiny of its Northern and Western neighbours.[1]

This is, in any case, just one of lines of study considered here; a line which deals with the effects that authoritarian rule can produce for the implementation of a more favourable ground for a durable taking root of democratic citizenship in certain Western societies. But another path for research is more original, one reason for it being that it is focused not on the past but on the present experiences of transition from authoritarianism to democracy. That is, on the direct "engineering" of democracy building exerted today by authoritarian political actors; even more crucially, on the responsibility which they sometimes keep of the management of the initial phase of the new democratic regime.

Even though Marshal Pildulski also believed in this idea in Poland during the 20's, Mustapha Kemal is probably the first modern dictator to have clearly said that he saw his authoritarian mandate as an obligation to guide a society—the Turkish society—towards democratic citizenship. When he states in front of the National Assembly, in 1926, "will it not be allowed that I conquer may own people" (Benoist-Mechin; 1954, 354), he is not manifesting anything else but this desire to force the conversion of the Turks—especially the rural masses—to a political modernity which many influences keep them from. For him, authoritarianism is only justifiable because it allows a provisory renunciation of compromise, in virtue of the fact that interests are not universalizable—therefore legitimately reconciliable—in a society which is still very segmented[2] Conversely, the tolerance of the expression of these interests would induce, during an indefinite period, not a democratic compromise but its very negation; that is, a conflictual climax without any other solution than that of a long authoritarian parentheses. As long as the antagonistic plurilegitimacy of segmentarian interests continues to predominate, it makes the unversalist recognition of democratic legitimacy of other types of interests counter—productive. However, this statement does not mean that the search for a democratic compromise has not to impose itself in an imperious fashion on the dictator, but only from the moment when segmentarian interests have ceased to dominate by the very fact of their being reduced to silence by the authoritarian phase.

But time is needed before this concept proper of philanthropic despots, marked like Pildulski, Mustapha Kemal, or Ismet Inonu by the progressive radicalism of their youth, penetrates the calculating minds of the old leaders of post World War II authoritarian regimes. Amongst the latter, the idea of a premeditated and controllable grant of democratic institutions insinuates itself by a detour which is very distant from Kemalist philanthropy. Because in their case, the motivation is no longer ideological but materialistic or economic and functional, in the same way as the planned implementation of the democratic "abertura" is no longer generous but strategic. In this perspective, the Spanish transition of 1975-1981 appears as a pragmatic illustration of a new authoritarian technology. A technology which delivers democracy ready-for-use, at the end of a planned operation conducted by a personnel essentially coming from the Francoist regime. Besides this it is almost immediately accepted as the prototype for modern democratization in recently industrialized societies struck until then by a sort of authoritarian fatality. The spanish model of democratization without discontinuance, without defeat and without drama imposes itself in contrast to the more accidented and revengeful "revolution des oeillets" in Portugal (where the voluntary conquest of liberty was nevertheless accompanied by an explicit right of arbitration of the army, and by a communist overbid which was contained at great cost). Henceforth, the Spanish model becomes the panacea not only in the eyes of the repentant or enlightened authoritarian leaders, but also in those of masses who are apprehensive of a possibly convulsive democratic change. Most often, it even convinces the leaders of the truly democratic opposition, who feel unsure of their forces and of the consequences to await from a risky confrontation with the established power.

Such is the tendency which characterizes many of the most recent and marking episodes of the extension of pluralist democracy. In 1978, Peruvian military, cured of the utopia of a martial revolution, already inspired themselves from the Spanish precedent without saying it. In 1979, their Ecuadorian colleagues, although more progressive, also proceeded towards a gradual and granted democratization. Above all, the Spanish democratic transition obviously inspired, in a recognized manner, the authoritarian strategies which resulted during 1983-1985 in the controlled restoration of representative regimes in Turkey, Uruguay and Brazil. Thus while at the same time, this model probably influences also the designs which can be which can be lent to the passably dictatorial leaders of a country as far away from Europe and Latin America as South Korea. Consequently, the second primordial axis of research on contemporary authoritarianism in newly industrialized societies penetrated by Western values appears clearly. It deals with the following question: are the non-communist mordernizing dictatorships in power in these societies the best builders of late democratic regimes?

Deficiencies and Partial Adequacies of the Theories of Authoritarianism.

It is true that this interrogation is valid but as a prolongation of that which was enounced in the first place, with reference to the implementation, by authoritarian regimes, of the economic, political and social bases for the regular exercise of democratic citizenship. It is also true that the available scientific literature is of little help, in general, when the problem is to understand the socio-political product of the conservative authoritarian modernization as well as the mechanisms of granted democratisation (as it has recently taken place in Southern European and Latin American societies).

For instance, the already surpassed theories of political development, as illustrated by Daniel Lerner (1958) and his followers, propose only indicators of social mobilization which are not pertinent to the questions raised here. It being understood that their inadequacy is not only that which they are often attributed. That is, to be based on an ethnocentric prejudice with emphasizes a Western type political dynamic as the only way offered to the nations of the world in their quest for modernity. Even though they were harmed for a long time by authoritarianism and if they are sometimes still, South European and Latin American societies are essentially Western, particularly because of their common partnership in a cultural co-tradition of European origin. Moreover, they often constitute areas already heavily touched by industrialization and urbanization. In many cases, they even experienced truncated but at the same time real democratic experiments, in spite of countercoups which ended them. Then, the insufficiency of these theories does not arise from the fact that late authoritarian democratization is quite normally referred to the Western model. In is a direct result of the ingenuousness of the indicators applied to West itself. Amongst the societies of the Southern Europe or America, many attained already, a few decades ago, levels of urbanization, literacy, relative equality of living conditions or even of political experience which surpassed those which their Northern neighbours enjoyed in the 19th century. So, if the relative deficiencies underlined by these indicators assume a reason, they signify not only that the societies from the South of the Western sphere lacked until recently the resources required for the enlargement of political participation. They also mean that those of the North found themselves, a hundred years before, in an identical situation . . . This, when they were precisely starting on the path towards their own democratic future . . . Speaking seriously, these indicators show not the impossibility of democracy in certain cases, but the contingency of their political corollaries in terms of democratic or authoritatian option. Probably this one is the most reasonable conclusion . . .

Similarly, the revision that Samuel P. Huntington (1968) carries out of the developmentalist schema is barely more operative. The problem about it does not arise from his idea that the institutionalization of channels of social mobilization represents the capital element of political stability. But Huntington neglects the problem raised here in supposing in advance that it is solved. For him, "the most important distinction among countries concerns not their form of government but their degree of government. The differences between democracy and dictatorship are less than the differences between those countries whose politics embodies consensus, community, legitimacy, organization, effectiveness, stability, and those countries whose politics is deficient in these qualities" (Huntington: 1968, 1). In the name of this unique functional cleavage which leaves no place for notions as formal as democracy and authoritarianism, he invalidates the efforts to pinpoint the specific products of authoritarian regimes. By the way, he postulates that the edification of institutional-structures is almost given in industrial nations, while the real situation is very different. Authoritarianism, which exists all the same in industrialized and non-industrialized societies, often tends to compensate for the deficiency of institutionalized agents of social control, either by substituting itself for all of them or by trying to accommodate them to its own goals.

In another direction, culturalist sociology of the Weberian tradition is no more of help to the present day researchers. In this regard, it appears only that Max Weber discerns without a doubt the politically modernizing role of Bonapartism or Bismarckism, specially when he calls them plebiscitarian democracies rather than semi-dictatorships. For Weber (1968, 268), these plebiscitarian democracies, close in fact to authoritarianism, do constitute one of the paths to the legal-rational modernisation of the Western State. But because of this, he considers a relatively old form of government; in any case, a political arrangement which is quite distinct from the technocratic dictatorships of the middle of the present century, whose plebiscitary ambitions are not the dominant feature because they claim above all a non-popular legitimacy of the governmental efficiency and of the economic performance.

But there fortunately exist more fruitful paths of reflection, often indirectly suggested by other works. Thus, when Stein Rokkan establishes a link between the rise of Fascism and the historical specificity of Central and Southern European countries; countries which were almost all hurt by the obstacles that the Holy Roman Germanic Empire, then the Hapsburg Empire, opposed during centuries to their emergence as centralized states and unified nations. In these contexts, authoritarianism would have represented an expeditive remedy to a delayed national and political construction (Rokkan Hagvett: 1980, 131-152). Besides, it could have played the same role for the emergence of post-World War II technocratic authoritarian regimes, no less preoccupied than their predecessors to bring an urgent solution to this same type of deficiency, born from more distant consequence—in the case of Latin America—of the imperial phenomenon. In this perspective, the analysis of the birth of authoritarianism fuses with that of its ends, which are to be observed as their socio-political product.

The works of Adam Przeworski (1975: 49-67) should also be considered for implicitly stressing a research hypothesis which deals with the long term political effects of delayed electoral mobilization. His frame of reference is certainly contestable, as far as this author makes Great Britain an electorally precocious country when universal suffrage isn't implemented there until 1918; and on the other hand, because the places Germany among the cases of late mobilization of the electorate when the universality of male suffrage is proclaimed there half a century earlier . . . But Przeworski is less interested by the formal aspect of electoral franchise than by its political results, in terms of the stakes which are really capable of motivating a large mass of voters (*i.e.*, by convincing it that the ballots have a real weight on political decisions). Now indeed, it is a fact that the strong state of Bismarckian tradition lessened, until 1918, the stakes of the German elections; or that, in a different manner, the clientelistic schemes denatured the parliamentary state until 1922-1923 in Italy or in Spain (even today in many Latin American countries).

For Przeworski, this loss in the meaning of voting thwarts democratic mobilization. In turn, moreover, the delayed electoral mobilization contributes to the weakness and the instability of government in the societies that it affects. It justifies, in particular, many authoritarian interventions facilitated by the indifference of the masses to the constantly ridiculed rules of democracy. At this point, the genetic interpretation of authoritarianism joins that of its modernizing strategies which interests us here. Often, the dictatorships which have arisen in this context of delayed mobilization had in view to carry out a complete refurbishing of corrupt political systems. In the case of fascist regimes, this design implied, in principle, a strategy of complete rupture with the past and of creation of a "New Man." But in the Post-World War II era, it redefined itself as a simple authoritarian recasting project of the bases of political socialization and political interplay. In short, in a plan which put politics between parentheses for an indeterminate length of time, in order to allow the concentration of all efforts on a preliminary rearrangement of an economic background, capable at last of supporting the ulterior return to a consensual power which can only be democratic nowadays. In these post-1945 authoritarian regimes, the temporary contempt of consensus represented just the indispensable expedient to the maintaining of an artificial stability capable of leading to a superior political order; a more solid order, which should sustain itself this time on the democratically institutionalized expression of expectations which would become tolerable from a population appeased by material progress.

Even though it is quite difficult to demonstrate it, also very suggestive is the paradigm which links the logic of the types of government of Western societies with the successive phases of industrialization. Certainly, one has to agree with David Landes (1975) that the industrial take-off of these societies accommodated itself to extremely varied political regimes: representative in Great Britain, Belgium and the United States; marked by a democratic-bonapartist alternance in France; and more clearly authoritarian in Germany, Russia, or later in Spain and Brazil. But Landes notes however that State intervention is inversely proportional to the degree of economic advancement of the country touched by the industrial take-off. The State has little place in societies where the rapid industrial development consolidates in itself thanks to the initiative of thousands of small and autonomous entrepreneurs, as in England or in Belgium. On the contrary, it plays a decisive role as promoter of industrialization when this takes place later on, because of the relative deficiency of these entrepreneurs. From which the differentiations, at once economic, technological and political, that Alexander Gershenkron (1962) suggests between the first two phases of industrialization: on the one hand, that of the "liberal-textile" industrialization of the British, where the momentum is given by dispersed private economic agents who spontaneously adjust their interests in the political framework of a transparent and relatively equalitarian game; on the other hand, the delayed "Steel and Iron industrialization" in the French and above all German style, where the amount of investments required for the economic take-off which takes place half a century later than in England makes that the economic initiative almost necessarily comes from the State and the big banks rather from private individuals. In this second case, the transparency of parliamentary politics disturbs the accommodation of the interests of these new actors who are much stronger than the small and medium entrepreneurs of the first phase of industrialization. This, because they have to resist the hostility of these more modest entrepreneurs who fear being taken for granted, and because the concentration of the steel and iron market—which concerns at the start armaments, ship-building and railroads—requires discrete arrangements between the rulers, the upper level civil servants and the big financiers.

Karl De Schweinitz (1964) develops this idea by placing the accent on the particular difficulties of democracy building in countries which do undertake their industrial expansion only during the second half of the 19th century or at the start of the 20th. Countries which, like Germany or Russia and Japan, have to jump over the textile phase in order to attain the steel and iron industrialization phase. De Schweinitz thinks that, in these cases, the size of the investments to mobilize and the obstacles to overcome require such a large intervention of the State that it almost implies the recourse to authoritarian or semi-authoritarian governments. This, not only owing to the amount of funds to be mobilized, but also because of the need for a direct and free communication (*i.e.*, ignoring the parliamentary representation) between the economic and the political-administrative elite. When the industrial take-off takes place only at the moment of the second "Steel and Iron phase," it conciliates itself better with the authoritarian technocracy-before the word—than with parliamentary democracy or predemocracy.

James Kurth (1979, 1-34) and David Collier (1978, 593-614) only update this interpretation by adapting it to the present context of late industrialization and its political counterparts. According to them, the countries which start industrializing themselves since 1945, like Spain and Brazil, obviously do it during an even later phase than that of the "State Steel and Iron industrialization" of the end of the 19th century. A phase which they qualify as "late rate" or "automotive," in order to distinguish it form the late industrialization of Bismarckian Germany or, to a certain extent, of France under the Second Empire. This third wave of industrialization has a number of elements in common with the "State Steel and Iron industrialization" phase. As with this phase, it needs a significant and concentrated mobilization of capital. It also requires a strong push by the State, the development of a public industrial sector palliating the lack of private initiative, the tightening of customs protection; likewise, the establishment of a direct and stable dialogue between a political administrative elite, which has become frankly technocratic, and an entrepreneurial elite which isn't any less so. By consequence, the continuity and the privacy of a modernizing authoritarian power are, in these societies, better suited to this project than the hazards and indiscretions of a representative regime. On the one hand, they help the authoritarian exercise of decision-making keeping away from the dangerous dialogue with the radical politicians who exalt worker's actions susceptible of lessening the comparative advantage which the new industries enjoy in a barely unionized environment. On the other, the authoritarian technocracy permits to marginalize the old traditional landed elite, whose interests are largely opposed to those of the new industrializing class and which could mobilize against it the old clientelistic electoral resource. In that way, authoritarianism gives the necessary time for the rearrangement of the summits of society, in the perspective of a more balanced fusion of the elite; it also guarantees to keep the low salaries which permit the quick industrial rise, for as long as possible.

But this third wave of industrialization, presents simultaneously notable difference with the second one. Differences which gradually contradict the authoritarian logic of its initial management, and leads to the search for a planned democratization formula. On the one hand, the capital needs can no longer, be essentially satisfied by the State; in the conditions of the present century, they have to be complemented by the multinationals more sizable and efficient investments. On the other hand, and contrary to the "State Steel and Iron industrialization" phase, the "Automotive Industrialization" phase tends to address itself no longer to a concentrated market depending above all on orders from the State (naval industry, armaments, and railroads); it depends on the very fragmented market of mass consumption (automobiles, durable consumer goods).

These differences foster three processes which are contrary to the survival of authoritarian regimes. The least important is linked to the multinationals, whose decision centres are in democratic societies (they find increasing difficulty to justify their connivance with the industrializing dictatorships). The second process concerns as much the multinationals as the big local entrepreneurs. It proceeds from the consciousness of the social tensions and the insufficient political outlets generated by the authoritarian policy of repression of the popular demands. Authoritarianism impedes the direct negotiation between employers and workers. In so doing, it blocks the emergence of unionized representatives that employers would like to see appear. In slowing the increases in salaries, it provokes, moreover, a stagnation in the standard of living which slows down the commercialization of industrial production, and orients it towards exports of finished products to already strongly industrialized countries where this competition is not necessarily welcome. Finally, the third process is the most difficult to isolate but also the most decisive. In the same manner as the arrival of mass consumption coincided with the democratic stabilisation of Western Europe after 1945, especially in Germany and in Italy it appears capable of also causing in other societies a sort of social satisfaction, able to dissolve the typical tensions of anterior democratic experiences. From that moment, "consumption democracy" (Hermet: 1983, 227-231) becomes liable to no nourish a consensus in the new industrializing societies of the 70's. It seems capable of guaranteeing the access to a higher level of political stability than that which is imposed with more and more difficulty by the authoritarian regimes. Henceforth also, the most enlightened authoritarian leaders can conceive that they would put the finishing touches on their task in channeling themselves this democratic stabilizing process. This process is designated here by the term "granted democratization."

To end this brief summary, it should be added that the dynamics of authoritarian democratization hypothetically suggested by Kurth and Collier can be linked to another medium range theory elaborated by Juan Linz and Alfred Stepan in their study of *The Brekdown of Democratic Regimes* (Linz, Stepan: 1978). Assuredly, these authors analyze not only the transition from authoritarianism to democracy but also its opposite: that is, the errors in political strategy and the miscalculations in the political agenda which contributed to the collapse of representative governments and to dictatorial interventions in Europe or in Latin America. However, this taking into consideration of the failed or erroneous strategies clearly indicates a line of research on granted democracy, as it takes place today. In fact, this mechanism translates the ambition of "democrats" without conviction, which the authoritarian technocrats are, to master the technology of democratic construction much better than the convinced democrats who failed before. Or rather, this ambition is accompanied by another sport of conviction: that of the legitimacy of competence, including when it stoops to conquer in front of the rival hardcore democratic legitimacy . . .

The Socio-political product of present day conservative authoritarian democratization

How should the socio-political product of post World War II conservative authoritarian modernization be evaluated? In this respect, one has to first consider the internal logic and the general orientation of the new type of authoritarian regimes which put it into place in the Iberian peninsula.

Compared to the preceding dictatorial rulers, the authoritarian "technocrats" who appear in Franco's Spain at the end of the 50's share nothing in common with the idealistic, philanthropic dictators of the Mustapha Kemal type. Political regimes are seen by them as accidental government formulas; amongst these dictatorship and democracy, whose merits are only to be measured in terms of their efficiency in assuring the continuity of material progress and of social cohesion in a given society. But these civilian technocrats, who reshuffle a Francoist dictatorship which until then was simply repressive, and who later on have imitators in Brazil and other countries, do not participate any more in fascist syndromes. This is obvious for what respects the racist element. Racist repression does not exist at all in the authoritarian regime reshaped by the Spanish or Portuguese technocrats; and it is very different and hidden in the Brazilian case (as in other Latin-American cases). The difference also imposes itself for what concerns the into-oligarchic setting of Fascism. At the outset, the Fascist pressure is largely due to the political frustration of middle classes deprived of power by the established elite. That is to say, to their desire of governing in their own name—be it in renouncing the electoral mechanism—rather than in the framework of parliamentary regimes where they occupied, in their eyes, a too limited place in front of the nobility and the professional political demagogues (Bauer: 1967). Technocratic authoritarianism does not partake at all in this anti-oligarchic attitude. If the authoritarian technocrats shake up the traditional oligarchy, it is only to force certain obstacles toward a reasonable conservative modernization, not by overall hostility to the oligarchic principle or because of some sort of petit-bourgeois ambition. In this perspective, their design consists only in modifying the balance of power between dominant groups; this in such a way that the traditional landed "gentry" ceases to dominate the new private and public entrepreneurial class, and gradually integrates itself into a fused elite, to which the modern leading class will give the tone.

In the same way, the authoritarian technocrats have not the intentions of imperialist territorial expansion which were typical of the fascist powers of the 30's; even less their spirit of militarist bellicosity. And no less essential are the differences which separate modernizing authoritarianism of technocratic inspiration from the populist strategies of Mussolini's dictatorship and above all, certain forms of Latin American authoritarianism. Mussolini flattered his popular supports by qualifying Italy "Nazione proletaria"; similarly Getulio Vargas used even more the direct appeal to a popular mobilization destined to comfort his charisma of providential leader in pre-1954 Brazil (with an aim which was, however, nothing but conservative, because it sought first of all to ensure the preservation of the existent agrarian structure at the price of a new clientelistic demagoguery).

The political practice of the technocratic phase of the Francoist regime exactly shuns this demagoguery, to the extent that it is frankly politically demobilizing. To an even greater extent, the civil and military leaders of post 1964 Brazilian dictatorship repudiate the populist manipulation (in saying that Vargas halted the industrial expansion of his country by granting a privileged status to the small industrial working class, with the sole desire to refurbish a different type of pseudo-democracy, based on acclaim rather than on the previously used electoral fraud). For the authoritarian Brazilian leaders, the goal of industrialization is much more important than the agrarian conservatism of the large landowners. And it implies that the populist appeal is not only abandoned, but condemned as the sin of political demagoguery, lack of national sense and social irresponsibility. More generally, the Spanish, Brazilian or Portuguese—of President Caetano's period—authoritarian technocrats keep with the anonymity of a rational bureaucratic legality which excludes all temptation of moving towards the building of a personal or collective political charisma.

At the same time, they use the nationalist and xenophobic resource with moderation uncommon in the authoritarian exercise of power. In fact, the model offered as an example to the populations they govern is that of highly industrialized Western societies. In this framework, their nationalism favours competition with these societies for access to industrial power, but not a direct confrontation which would not further this major goal. Also in this framework, anti-American and anti-European xenophobia becomes a hindrance, because the goal is precisely to align oneself with the "Gringos." Thus, there is only one external evil left to be designated to public condemnation: that is, communism, which is presented as the great enemy of national progress. This in the light of an exercise of power which avoids, however, presenting itself as counter-revolutionary or as purely militaristic. Modernizing technocratic authoritarianism avoids the use of force. It prefers to it the promise of a material well-being to come. It breaks also with the traditional military regimes: first, to the extent that it tries to institutionalize itself in a legality which becomes civilian in its form if not in its most influential agents; equally, or even more so, because it wants to be the founder of a new long-term social dynamics.

The positive nature of authoritarian conservative modernization henceforth sketches itself. This form of authoritarianism replaces the philanthropic prejudice of the idealistic dictators by a positivist or materialistic prejudice. For the authoritarian technocrats, the progress of societies and their adjustment to a freer citizenship depends chiefly on the transformation of the material conditions of life, in terms of satisfaction of existing and future needs as well as in terms of lifestyle in general. The initiator of the second modernizing phase of the Francoist regime, Laureano Lopez Rodo, sets the tone in this regard when he declares in substance: "what is most important is to reach a per capita rent of 1000 dollars per year; all the rest, including democracy, will come in addition."

Used next by the "colonels regime" in Greece, then by the minister Delfim Netto in Brazil, this brief formulation means that industrialization conditions societal change: In the name of the positivist voluntarism which also characterizes the action of the technocrats, it implies, moreover, that industrial development can only take place in accordance with the only model which has until now proven itself: that a competitive capitalist industrialization which doest not exclude, at the outset, a certain amount of protectionism. But this materialistic project with a superior goal does not imply that this goal—a possible democratic outcome?—has to be enounced in advance. On the one hand, the search for power and national stability counts at least as much as the democratic product which may accompany it; if it should consolidate itself at the end of the industrializing process, democracy remains but one type of government amongst others, whose main merit resides not in its intrinsic but in its symbolic value, as a sign of belonging to the community of advanced industrialized societies. On the other hand, a premature announcement of the democratization goal would risk to hurt the industrialization dynamic by giving birth to uncontrollable popular expectations and too explicit fears in the oligarchy. At the start, the indispensable industrialization forcedly allies against it diverse formidable enemies, from the working class reduced for a period of time to a congruous place to the always strong groups of the traditional oligarchy, poorly treated in their landed domination and threatened to be taken for granted in a new balance of the elites. Consequently, it reveals itself hardly compatible with the immediate search of a consensus. The discretionary power that the technocrats claim of exert possesses, in their eyes, its legitimacy: that of competence and of economic efficiency. And it excludes that they make an appeal to a wider legitimacy which would sap their eminent power. The technocrats must mask their advances, including towards democracy.

Simultaneously, the technocratic authoritarian project is in Reeping with a functional or systemic logic. It postulates the feedback: that is, the gradual modification of demands and attitudes under the impact of more and more positive responses which they are given at the material level, due to industrial expansion. Henceforth, the idea is that the economic demands of the previously critical sectors of society should rationally become less pressing and destabilizing. Better still, this idea is also such that the demands of a more political or statutory nature should in turn diminish. The bet, then, is to postulate that the responses given to the economic demands of the masses will progressively convince them that they have some tangible interests to care for, and that the advantages thus acquired might become vulnerable in the case of a brutal political crisis. In short, the technocrats think that the gradual arrival of the age of mass consumption should divert the urban working class, enlarged by rural migration, from its previous tendency to an all or nothing attitude of revolutionary idealism.

In this way, the technocratic authoritarian design acquires one of its last characters, which touches on its fundational dimension. Because, if the feedback constitutes the instrument of adaptation and maintenance of the social system, it can contribute also to the necessary change of the political apparatus, specially at the moment when authoritarianism appears more and more poorly adapted to the selection of popular demands; when it even becomes harmful for what respects the relationship between the political power and its environment. Finally, the technocrats can happen to consider themselves authoritarianism as a political nuisance, whose value was only linked, at a given moment, to its capacity to cut the communication between the industrializing State and its hostile or incomprehensive environment. In virtue of which these "political entrepreneurs" also think, that this kind of lock-out cannot be used as a long term formula; in other words, that authoritarian power is good only to prepare the ground for a less artificial political stability, resting this time on an enlarged intercommunication and a more flexible choice vis-a-vis the popular demands. In this way, technocratic authoritarianism pretends to assume the constituent or foundational role we referred to before. It being understood that the constitution in question has nothing to do with a formal political charter. What matters, indeed, is to work to the birth of a "social constitution" able of really supporting solid representative institutions.

Finally, the last character of the authoritarian conservative modernization is based on its latent "mesocratic" principle. There is no doubt that the technocrats keep being indifferent to the formal nature of governments, whose quality is linked in their eyes to their efficiency rather than to their conformity to an ideology. And they have only contempt for democratic speeches which seem to seek at the same time one thing and its opposite (in promising well-being, while simultaneously refusing to conceive the social costs of the industrialization which makes it possible). Above all, they conceive their industrializing project as the mean of a dynamics of expansion of durable consumer goods production. Technologically, this dynamics supposes that a sufficient retribution will the be granted to its main agents, who belong to the middle class in general. Economically, this material incentive creates at the same time the take-off market for these consumer goods, even though they remain inaccessible to the masses for a little while longer. Then, the authoritarian conservative modernization first favours the intermediary stratum of the population. Moreover, it does not favour only the material demands of this category, but also the appearance of post-material expectations in this group. Amongst these expectations: the need for information unbiased by censors, later on that of a more mature political status for the middle classes. In this manner, the authoritarian technocrats try, in sum, to channel the claim for democracy, in order to transform it into a mesocratic impulse capable of winning over a destructive and indifferentiated popular pressure.

In view of these more or less expressed intentions and of these inferred rather than proclaimed strategic aims, it is not easy to evaluate the effective social product of authoritarian conservative modernization. Furthermore, this evaluation would require a statistical analysis which exceeds the scope of this purely methodological contribution. At this level, it suffices to enounce the paths which appear to be the most significant for the elucidation of this product.

The agrarian malaise, which until now heavily weighed on the political destiny of countries such as Brazil or Spain, should be considered first. The anti-democratic fatality nourished itself in these countries of the backwardness of peasant societies, marked both by the weight of the clientelistic domination and by outbursts of anarchist or millienaristic revolts. Can it be believed that authoritarian conservative modernization modifies these situations, to such an extent that this agrarian element ceases to perdominate? The example of Great Britain—as well as those of many other European countries besides France—clearly illustrates that democracy is not born from agrarian reform. On the contrary, democracy made this reform useless, to the extent that the political mobilization could rely very quickly on a population which became urban in its majority. In the same fashion, does authoritarian conservative modernization contribute to remove the spectre of a large peasant uprisal which had frightened a long time the friends of democracy? Does it reduce the agrarian problem, until then primordial, to the rank of a simple economic problem (*i.e.*, no longer structural), compatible with something like an undramatized democratic management? The answer to this question is certainly positive in the case of Spain and even Portugal. But it appears much more doubtful in the case of Brazil, in spite of the large transfer of population which took place between the rural states of the North-east or the Center and the industrial regions in the South. It is well known, indeed, that the peasant exodus requires a long period of social digestion, and that it can sometimes result in ruralizing the cities, by transferring the old agrarian revolt rather than emptying the rural areas of their excess workers. . .

The analysis of the growth of industrialized urban centers permits to pinpoint the other side of the same process. But the question is not only, in this perspective, to define the relative evolution of large masses of population by the type of residence and by sector of activity. First of all, it is necessary to understand two phenomena which are more specific in their political impact. The first deals with the organization of the elites and with the respective weight of the old landholding oligarchy and the new modernizing elite; in other words, to what we can perceive of it, beyond the large statistical aggregates. In order to operate really, the technocratic authoritarian project must force the resistance of the traditional oligarchy. For this, a shake-up in the relationship between the old and new elite is required. Moreover, a triter aspect to be dealt with concerns the internal composition of the urban masses, in particular the degree of their integration in the industrial cycle and the modern wage-earning class. When these masses still include a great proportion of largely unemployed ex-peasants, or unskilled workers whose precarious subsistence depends on the goodwill of the State, it is worth betting on that they do not supply yet the base for a really new political reformulation. On the contrary, the insertion of the urban masses into a permanent wage-earning status and a relatively affluent consumers milieu permits to foresee the opposite with regard to the reconfiguration of the elites as well as that of urban populations, it shows through again that the very reality of it appears more dubious in the case of the Brazilian military regime than in the case of the Francoist dictatorship (more so, to be true, at the level of the unfinished mass urbanization than for what respects the equilibrium at the top, which is better marked today by the emergence of a modern leadership).

Other elements should of course be taken into account in order to grasp the social impact of technocratic authoritarianism. Thus its cultural product in terms of education and reduction of illiteracy (because the post-authoritarian political "abertura" finds itself contradictorily influenced by the general progress of education and by the tension created by the premature arrival of the labour market of literate or even high school educated unemployed). However, the consideration of the direct political product of this form of authoritarianism imposes itself more on the spirit. In this respect, the technocratic dictatorships do not accelerate only the social changes which modify the social background of democracy building. They can also transform the very political elements of this construction.

On this point, the electoral practice of these dictatorships weighs much less than those of certain European semi authoritarian regimes of the 19th century. The second Empire banalized universal suffrage in France and Bismarck installed it in Germany. This was not the case in Spain, where the non-competitive elections organized by the Francoist regime (Hermet: 1974) left no mark, to say nothing of the Portuguese elections prior to 1974 or those held in Iran at the time of the Shah (Hermet, Rose, Rouquie: 1978). On its side, if the post 1964 military regime introduced forced bipartism in Brazil, all lead one to think that such a system has only a few chances to survive the return to free elections in this country.

But on the other hand, there is no doubt that the authoritarian technocrats brought a decisive contribution to the eradication of pre-existing party systems and political groups. In so doing, they removed some of the obstacles which blocked until then the development of a democratic practice liberated from clientelistic influences as well as from libertarian or messianic impulses. This is particulary the case in Spain, where the long Francoist episode clearly contributed to the elimination of a long anarchist domination on the worker's movement, and prepared the way for social democracy. This is also what happened in Portugal, where, 45 years of dictatorship led to the withering away of the traditional political oligarchy, and paved way for the emergence of a new party system dominated by the Socialists. In return, the Brazilian example remains ambiguous once more. If the military shook up the tripartism left by Getulio Vargas, this system seems to resurge out of its shambles. But it is also true that it does not dispose any longer of the same clientelistic resources, and that populist demagoguery gets by less easily in today's Brazil. The question is, therefore, to see whether the multipartisan reorganization represents just a rebirth of the old tripartism, or is, on the contrary, a real reconstruction of the framework offered to the expression of democratic citizenship in Brazil other. In this regard, the modernizing fusion of the elites carried out during the phases of technocratic authoritarianism can settle a powerful factor of political renovation. On the one hand, this fusion implies that the traditional oligarchy ceases to exert its "patronage" on the political competition, and is forced consequently to retreat into a residual political space. On the other, the same integration process involves a unified political socialization of elites which consolidates the communication between their formerly antagonistic groups. This type of socialization transcends the partisan or ideological cleavages and creates a common language, capable of nullifying the manichean antagonisms of previous political confrontations. Until then rejected because of incompatible allegiances, the legitimacy of compromise and of the necessary reference to an uncorrupted universal suffrage has to be accepted by the historically reluctant fraction of the elites. Here again, the example of Spain comes to mind, as it is a well known fact that the Francoist era facilitated the establishment of new bases for dialogue between the previously irreconcilable conservative and modern leaders. But it remains, however, that the positive reference to the socio-political product of the Spanish dictatorship leads to an interrogation. What, in this product, is based the very effects of the authoritarian conservative modernization strategy, and what is merely due to the numerous factors which operated because of the length of the dictatorial phase? In order to become foundational, dictatorships of all types probably need to last one generation at least. Without which they would not eliminate the previous political system, and only lead to a restoration of the democratic impasse which had justified the authoritarian intervention?

The Mechanics of Granted Democracy

It is true that the opposite argument arises right away. Including in Spain, the action of the authoritarian technocrats characterized but a relatively short fraction of 39 years of Francoist dictatorship: on the whole, the period which covers from 1960 to 1973. However, this fairly brief period of time sufficed for that the fundamental contradiction of the technocratic strategy of authoritarian modernization produced its self-destructive effect and induced the final tactics of granted democracy.

Consciously or not, the industrializing technocrats work not only toward a socio-economic change which settles more favourable conditions for an ulterior democratic stabilization. They also act as apprentice-sorcerers, in undermining at the same time the authoritarian power they are supposed to serve and the radical opposition which is normally supposed to be the agent of a future democratic change. In fact, the success of the technocratic strategy brings with it a systematic weakening of the dictatorial camp as well as of its declared opponents. It thus reinforces the probability of a planned democratic transition rather than of a real democratic rupture, which would be symbolized by the replacement of the authoritarian regime by a constituent representative regime.

The reason for this contradiction is that the process of accelerated industrialization conducted by the authoritarian technocrats generates transformations which are much deeper than those carried out by more classical dictatorships. Almost immediately, it causes a syndrome of social troubles similar to that which Albert Hirschman calls the tunnel effect. (Hirschman: 1978, 519-543). But the trouble is not limited, as Hirschman suggests, to the development of a growing intolerance before income inequality, which appears at the very moment when the progress of industrialization permits to see the exit of the long tunnel of poverty. In the case of already advanced Western societies, as those of Spain and Brazil,[3] the tunnel effect goes beyond the simple economic unhappiness. It is related to an overall malaise which tends to express itself politically. On the one hand, the middle classes nevertheless materially favoured by modernization aspire to satisfactions of another nature. To borrow again from Hirschman (1982), they cease to confine themselves on their selfish private interest, and begin to dream of public actions of a more philanthropic type (which the dictatorship cannot tolerate, in spite of its mesoratic dynamics in the long run). On the other hand, the working masses accept less and less to undergo the main cost of industrialization; this, at the moment when the load becomes less disproportionate for them, when the economic expansion finally solves the long time endemic unemployment, and when the progress in productivity allows some salary increases compatible with the maintenance of a certain comparative advantage. In this way the authoritarian conservative modernization increases the social pressure instead of reducing it. Having wanted to replace the big stick of open repression by the soft incentive of authoritarian welfare, the authoriarian industrializers find themselves confronted by the unpleasant hypothesis of a return to the big stick.

In a similar manner, the sudden modernization also feeds the increasing frustration of the traditional oligarchy and the stagnant sectors of society, notably amongst the small to medium size farmers. They all fear the changes which harm their habits, lower their social status, and oblige them to undertake difficult adaptations. Above all, the oligrachy protests against political changes which took place much to its surprise, even though they were generated by a dictatorship in which it considered itself as the majority shareholder. The industrial growth orchestrated by the technocrats weakens the bases of the old popular deference to the oligarchy; it erodes in an even more serious manner its previously dominant position in the authoritarian government. Once master of the political game, the oligarchy becomes a victim of the very hand which should have been committed to it. Combining itself with the previous elements of deterioration of the dictatorial equilibrium, this factor represents one of the many reasons which explain why the most successful authoritarian technocratic regimes see their support vanish at the very moment when their opponents become more conscious of their hostility toward them. (That is, when the positive result of the galloping industrialization policy, whose merit belongs to them, should have at least brought them a *satisfecit*). In a word, the cold rationality of the technocrats seems to ignore the ambivalence of human nature. And, as if by definition, this ignorance deprives them of the supports which dictatorships enjoy in more usual circumstances.

But this erosion of the authoritarian legitimacy does not have as a corrolary the reinforcement of the hardcore democratic opposition. Made unhappy by the barriers which the dictatorship impose on the expression of a free citizenship, but also anxious to preserving its recently increased standard of living, a large part of the population is fundamentally upset by the idea of a radical political change which could endanger economic acquisitions prized more than anything else. In this perspective, the rank and file of citizenry is aware of the precarity of his recent progress on the road to mass consumption, of the vulnerability of a relative private happiness which is not yet viewed is a right or as an indisputable fact. He dreads, in particular, that the jolts which often come along with the rebirth of democracy, at the end of a direct strife against a dictatorship, would get the better of his fragile gains. In newly industrialized societies, this is the reason why a large fraction of the population is only moderately democratic; in any case, not to the point of calling for a dramatized and resentful democratic rupture, in which the radical opposition would find an occasion for revenge. The opposite seems to be more accurate. In modernizing dictatorships near their end, which are always better than their preceding regimes as would have written Tocqueville, repression has become civilized. The inexpiable hatreds are no longer in fashion, to the extent that the risk of overthrow of the established power by force almost disappears. Moreover, one has to consider also that the technocratic dictatorships are pacific in general, thus hardly succeptible of falling apart after a military defeat as in the case of the Italian, German and Balkan or Argentine dictatorships.

In these circumstances, the best political odds are not with those who conceive of such an overthrow: that is to say, the leaders of the hardcore democratic opposition. This opposition refuses to compromise with even the liberal elements of the authoritarian regime, firm in its belief that this democracy should be conquered and not granted. It is attached also to the idea that the new regime should explicitly repudiate the one it just replaced, and take on a constituent character from the outset. A large part of the population exactly whishes the opposite: a painless and smooth transition to democracy . . .

This dissonance in the intentions singularly restricts the possibilities for action by the democratic counter elite. It constrains it either to a battle for honours's sake which is almost lost from the outset, or to an abjuration of its principles in view of a fairly impure agreement with the holders of power. In order to illustrate this fact, one only needs to remember the successive retreats of the Spanish Communist Party, once spearhead of the anti-Francoist fight during 39 years. Between 1974 and 1976, this party slipped from a democratic counter government project to that of a cabinet of national union, before finally ending up with the real choice of an unconditional support of the post-authoritarian planned democratization conducted by the ex-Francoist Prime Minister, Adolfo Suarez. Furthermore, what is true for the Spanish communists is also true for the socialists and other movements of the previously republican opposition. Similarly, the same statement is valid also for a large part of the democratic opposition 1984-1985 Brazil. The future President, Tancredo Neves, found himself opposed by the military with such an unlikely candidate, in the person of Paulo Maluf, that this election almost appeared as the result of a Machiavellian connivance between the military leaders and their pseudo-opponents, the moderate democrats. Moreover, these latter accommodated themselves very easily to the electoral rules—indirect ballot—imposed by the military; and, in the same fashion, the ex-opposition party—the PMDB generously welcomed the *transfugees* of the former official party (the ARENA, refurbished under the name of PDS). In a word, the strategy of authoritarian conservative modernization debilitates as the same time the dictatorship which it is supposed to serve, and the democratic groups which oppose it. In so doing, it induces the middle solution of planned democratic transition, under the guardianship of the modernizing sector of the authoritarian system.

After the death of President Neves, the boldness of the reforms initiated by President Jose Sarney clearly demonstrates that an heir to authoritarianism enjoys more liberty than a patented democrat for making rapid progress on the path towards democratization. Before him, Adolfo Suarez had shown that this liberty rested on the privileged control which he exerted over the army and the State apparatus, even more on the confidence he inspired in all those who were afraid of the change but accepted in from one of theirs. What would indeed appear as a policy of demagougie inspiration on the part of a leader coming from the democratic opposition can be received, in sum, as a proof of political cleverness or as a necessary move on the part of rulers who are warranted by their authoritarian past. . .

However, this hypothesis is obviously referred to the Spanish and Brazilian examples of granted democratization. For this reason, it is too axiomatic or too specific to offer the general framework for a comparative interpretation. In a more comprehensive perspective, these two cases need to be confronted to other processes of authoritarian democratization: for instance, those of post-war Turkey, of Ecuador and Peru from the end of the 70's, very recently of Uruguay and perhaps soon of South Korea.[4]

To do this, a short-range framework, capable of identifying at least the immediate examples of post-authoritarian democratization from above, is to be found. In this perspective, we will indeed just try to give here a few points of reference for the comparative study of this only immediate mechanism of democratic transition managed by ex-authoritarian rulers. Certainly, the socio-economic, cultural and political background of this type of democracy building has to be taken into account. But this basic consideration does not require any particular methodological proposal, because it belongs already to a well established political science or macro-sociological practice. And, on its side, if the final product of this form of democratization represents in an indisputable manner the most important question, it is still too early to answer it.

Consequently, the research work has to deal with what is now possible to analyze, and what is not yet an object of systematic interpretation: that is, the dynamics of granted democracy in the making. Even though they are insufficient, two criteria impose themselves in this regard: that of political zoning, and that of timing—or of the agenda—of the democratic transitions induced by authoritarian conservative modernization. The political zoning imposes itself first, because it makes possible, to intellectually locate the multiple political sites which are unequally retained, privileged or excluded during the planned democratic "aberturas." At this level, three initial variables—the first two variables are interdependent—concern the orientations of the authoritarian power in the anterior or preparatory phase to democratization:

(i) First, at the level of the exercise of authoritarian power which, even in a reputedly dictatorial regime, situates itself on different points of a vector going from a very authoritarian coercion to a liberal exercise (based on the allocation of satisfactions to the population and on actual compromise).

(ii) Next, at the level of the choice of leaders, which even in an authoritarian regime, locates itself in the same fashion, going from closed cooptation to semi-competitive election, passing through relatively open meritocratic cooptation (whitout excluding a democratic election with nothing at stake).

(iii) Finally, for what deals with the tolerance shown in the last few years by authoritarian leaders vis-a-vis the opposition leaders. The latter may have been victims of ostracization until the last day. But they may also have been readmitted before the end of the dictatorship. (Sometimes with the very obvious aim of preparing way for a future democratization, in giving some interlocutors to the leaders of the planned political "abertura").

On their side, the over variables apply to the democratic transition in itself, and relate in an inevitably banal manner to the numerous possible settings of the political liberalization. They concern particulary.

(iv) The composition of the governmental and upper administrative elite during the initial phase of the transition (to what extent does it come directly from the authoritarian apparatus; which groups of this milieu does it arise from?).

(v) The reality and quality of the elections (composition of the electoral body, type of baelot and degree of competition, real stakes of the elections).

(vi) The inclusiveness of the legally accepted political forces. At this level, the recognition of the extreme left and especially of the Communist Parties represent a touchstone; the authoritarian democrats generally refuse to accept them at the beginning; but many resolve to after diverse events. While others do not concede on this point and, in so doing, soil the democratic legitimacy of the transition.

(vii) The inclusiveness of the parallel spectrum of legalized trade unions and their real strength. The tolerance of trade unions can be greater than that of parties or vice versa. Furthermore, the placing under trusteeship of the worker's movement by the official labour unions of the previous authoritarian regime may have generated such a negative locking that it deprives the democratic government of strong union interlocutors (as in Brazil today). On the contrary, authoritarianism can have tolerated the gradual renaissance of semi-legal trade unions, which later on provide for well prepared representatives (as Spain, or Uruguay. . . .).

(viii) The restoration of political liberties in general, including the treatment given to old opponents (readmission on national territory, amnesty, exercise of civil rights, and the right to candidature. . .).

(ix) The social and economic management of the new democratic regime (pact vs.confrontation with the trade unions, price and salary controls, structural reforms, management of the external debt, tax policy, labour policy and management of unemployment. . .).

(x) The new regimes information policy (maintenance or not of the control exerted by the power on the media, in general).

Other elements could be pointed out. However, the comprehensiveness in this regard is less important than the relationship between this political zoning and the timing of the agenda of planned democratization. The once authoritarian "founding fathers" of granted democracy can play on the different settings of political "abertura" off each other; they may ignore those which they think still impracticable, the same as they can favor others supposed to be more controllable; they may conceive, for example, that it suffices during a certain time to restore the freedom of speech and the competition between moderate parties, without having for all that to lift the ban maintained against the communists. Above all, these successful or failed acts are almost inevitably realized according to a progressive and in each case different calendar. Almost by definition, granted democratization excludes the uniform and synchronized removal of all the barriers opposing a democratic spontaneity, susceptible of being confiscated by a radical counter elite suspected of irresponsibility. In this perspective, really free elections can be put off to a fairly distant future, as in Spain and Brazil. But they can also open the transition for reasons which remain to be discovered, as in Ecuador and Uruguay.

Similarly, the legal admission of communist parties rarely takes place right away, or is expressly refused as in Turkey. At all levels, a proportioning of democratic elements takes place in terms of both a preestablished design and of immediate circumstances. Finally, it appears that a good balance is struck when the adequation of political zoning to its timing reduces the legitimacy of the hardcore democratic opposition to a very residual role. Conversely, the operation fails when this opposition keeps at least an alternative legitimacy. Furthermore, granted democratization reaches its point of no return when the governing elite, issued for the most part from the previous authoritarian regime, legally hands the place over to a new democratic elite which does not give itself a constituent role. That is, when this new elite recognizes in so doing the value of the transition without rupture and the democratic merits of the institutions established in this context.

This outline of an interpretative scheme is worth what the very phenomenon of post-authoritarian democratization from above is on its side. This strategy has resulted in a significant performance in Spain. But such an honourable product does not mean that granted democratization imposes itself henceforth as a prevailing paradigm in the emergence of a new democratic modernity. On the other hand, this type of strategy seems to be extremely linked to the hazards of the economic circumstances (to the point of taking on the role, to a certain extent, of a political satisfaction conceded to a population, to which the authoritarian rulers can no longer offer material satisfactions because of the economic crisis). On the other hand, the most convincing examples of this strategy all concern countries which are globally impregnated with the values of Western culture. Until now, granted democratization has not proven itself in societies which do not have these two characteristics (if we exclude the very particular case of post-war Japan). Yet, these restrictions cannot contradict the fact that planned authoritarian "abertura" recently was the most significant phenomenon in the march toward democracy at the edges of the Western World. The political reality has to be analyzed even when it is rather dull. . .

NOTES

1. Or , in the case of East Germany, Naziism permitted its final a different to a fully totalitarian equalitarianism. . .

2. See Leca (1977, 572).

3. To be true, Hirschman is thinking of Pakistan or Nigeria rather than of Latin America or the Iberian Perinsula.

4 A reference could be made also to the more timid experiments in democratization carried out in Egypt, Tunisia, Morocco, or Senegal.

REFERENCES

Alber, Jens, (1976), *Participants in Social Insurance Systems in Western Europe*, Mannheim. HTWED Report.

Bagehot, Walter, (1964), *The English Constitution,* London. C,A. Walts (First edition: 1867).

Bauer, Otto, (1967), "Der Faschismus", in: Abendroth (W.) *et al.*, *Faschismus and Kapitalismus*, Europa Verlag.

Benoist-Mechin, J., (1954), *Mustapha Kemal ou la mort d'un empire*, Paris, Albin Michel.

Collier, David, (1978), "Industrialization and Political Change," *World Politics* (38), pp 593-614.

Dahrendorf. Ralf, (1962), *Society and Democracy in Germany*, Garden City, Anchor Books.

De Schweinitz, Karl Jr., 1964, *Industrialization and Democracy*, London, The Free Press of Glencoe.

Gerschenkron, Alexander, 1962, *Economic Backwardness in Historical Perspective*, Cambridge (Mass.), The Bellknap Press of Harvard University Press.

Hermet, Guy, 1974, "Electoral Trends in Spain: an Appraisal of the Pols conducted under the Franco Regime," *Iberian Studies* 8 (2); pp. 1-5.

Hermet G., *Rose*, R., *Rouquie* A., ed., 1978, *Elections without Choice*, London, The Macmillan Press.

Hermet, G., 1983, *Aux frontieres de la democratie*, Paris, Presses Universitaires de France.

Hirschman, Albert, 0., 1978, "The Changing Tolerance for Income Inequality in the Course of Economic Development," in: *Singh*, S.P., ed., *Underdevelopment to Developing Countries*, Bombay, Oxford University Press.

—1982, *Shifting Involvments: Private Interest and Public Action*, Princeton, Princeton University Press.

Huntington, Samuel P., (1968), *Political Order in Changing Societies*, New Haven, Yale University Press.

Kurth, James R., (1979), "The Political Consequences of the Product Cycle," *International Organization* 33 (1): pp. 1-34.

Landes David S., (1975), *The Unbound Prometheus. Technological Change and Industrial Development in Western Europe*, London, Cambridge University Press.

Leca Jean, (1977), "Pour une analyse comparative des systemes politiques mediterraneens," *Revue francaise de science politique* 27 (4.5), pp. 557-581.

Lerner Daniel, (1958), *The Passing of Traditional Societies*, Glencoe, The Free Press.

Linz Juan J., (1964), "An Authoritarian Regime: Spain," in Allardt (E.), Littunen (Y.), ed., *Cleavages, Ideologies and Party Systems*, Helsinki, The Academic Bookstore.

Linz Juan J., *Stepan,* Alfred, ed., (1978), *The Breakdown of Democratic Regimes*, Baltimore, The Johns Hopkins University Press.

Moore Barrington Jr., (1966), *Social Origins of Dictatorship and Democracy*, Boston, Beacon Press.

Neumann, Franz, 1957, *The Democratic and the Authoritarian State*, Glence, The Free Press.

Przeworski Adam, (1975), "Institutionalization of Voting Patterns or is Mobilization the Source of Decay," *American Political Science Review* 69 (1): pp. 49-67.

Siegfried, Andre, (1913), *Tableau politique de la France de l'Ouestsous la Troisieme Republique*, Paris, Armand Colin.

Vajda, Mihaly, (1975), *Fascisme et mouvement de masse*, Paris Le Sycomore.

Weber, Max, (1968), *Economy and Society*, New York, Bedminster Press, vol. 1.